Anthology of
Modern Indonesian Poetry

ANTHOLOGY OF

Modern
Indonesian
Poetry

edited by

Burton Raffel

UNIVERSITY OF CALIFORNIA PRESS · 1964

Berkeley and Los Angeles

University of California Press
Berkeley and Los Angeles

Cambridge University Press
London, England

kepada isteriku,
Helen, jang mengakibatkan
semua mungkin

ACKNOWLEDGMENTS

THIS VOLUME was sponsored by the Publications Program of the Asia Society. Mrs. Bonnie R. Crown, Publications Director of the Society, has forbidden me to do more than say thank you for the enormous amount of help she has given. Her assistant, Miss Susan Conheim, has frequently been my assistant too, during the three years it has taken to complete the book.

My principal debts for advice, assistance of all sorts, books, and what-have-you, must at least be mentioned. Portions of the manuscript have been read and helpfully commented upon by Mr. Boyd Compton, Mr. S. Takdir Alisjahbana, Mr. Derwent May, Mr. H. B. Jassin, Mr. Mohammad Akbar Djuhana, and Mr. James S Holmes. The entire volume was examined by Professor John M. Echols, of Cornell University's Department of Far Eastern Studies. Professor Echols has also been continually on call for everything from biographical data to the meanings of obscure Indonesian locutions. (His and Mr. Hassan Shadily's *An Indonesian-English Dictionary*, first published in 1961, has proved to be one of the most valuable books in my *kumpulan buku-buku Indonesia*.) Soedjatmoko, Director of P. T. Pembangunan, and Subagio Sastrowardojo, of Gadjah Mada University, allowed me to profit from their immense learning and good judgment; Mr. Soedjatmoko very kindly supplied me with a copy of *Basis* (Jogjakarta), containing invaluable material on W. S. Rendra. The guidance afforded me by Mr. Nurdin Salam, of Makassar, once my student and long my collaborator, has been indispensable; the books and other materials he has sent me, over the years, are the foundation on which this book rests. One of my chief regrets has been that distance and the difficulties of communication prevented Mr. Salam from sharing editorial responsibilities with me. Clearly, it would have been a better book had I been able to rely on him, day by day, in the many areas he knows far more intimately than I can ever hope to.

The translation of Mohammad Akbar Djuhana's "Poète Maudit" included in this anthology was first published in Professor Ahmed Ali's *The Flaming Earth* (Karachi, 1949), and is reprinted here by Professor Ali's generous permission. The Dutch original of the poem was kindly supplied by Professor A. Teeuw, of Leiden. My last debt is also my greatest: to my wife, Helen, for knowing Indonesian better than I do, and for cheerfully making her knowledge and good taste available to me, in spite of the demands of her own very active professional career.

My translators—I hope they will allow me the possessive, here—have been a pleasure to work with. We have worked, no doubt about it; the results are not ours to judge, but I hope they have found the labor as rewarding and enriching as I have. (Brief summaries of their careers are given on pages 156–158.) As editor, I have made it my invariable rule to compare every English version submitted to me with its Indonesian original, line for line and word for word. Where my suggestions have exceeded an editorial minimum, the translation is usually described as a collaborative effort. In a few cases translator and editor have agreed to disagree on details; otherwise I am as responsible as any of the other translators if errors have persisted—and even more responsible, since it was my job to prevent just such errors.

* * *

My thanks to Pustaka Rakjat (publishers of Amir Hamzah, Sutan Takdir Alisjahbana, Chairil Anwar's *Kerikil Tadjam* and his *Jang Terampas dan Jang Putus*, and Sitor Situmorang's *Surat Kertas Hidjau*); to Balai Pustaka (publishers of Aoh Kartahadimadja, and of the tripartite volume *Tiga Menguak Takdir*, by Chairil Anwar, Rivai Apin, and Asrul Sani); to P. T. Pembangunan (publishers of Chairil Anwar's *Deru Tjampur Debu*, Sitor Situmorang's *Wadjah Tak Bernama*, Toto Sudarto Bachtiar's *Etsa*, W. S. Rendra, and Ajip Rossidhy); to Penerbit Gunung Agung (publishers of H. B. Jassin's *Chairil Anwar, Pelopor Angkatan 45*); to

viii

Badan Musjawarat Kebudajaan Nasional (publishers of Toto Sudarto Bachtiar's *Suara*); and, finally, to the publishers of three anthologies from which poems have been drawn: Pustaka Rakjat (for Sutan Takdir Alisjahbana's *Puisi Baru*), Penerbit IQBAL (for Bakri Siregar's *Penjair dan Sandjak*), and Balai Pustaka (for H. B. Jassin's *Gema Tanah Air*).

Some of these translations have appeared in *Prairie Schooner, The Beloit Poetry Journal, Poetry Northwest, The Texas Quarterly, Perspective of Indonesia* (in *The Atlantic,* June, 1956), and in John M. Echols' *Indonesian Writing in Translation.* Most of the versions of Chairil Anwar's poetry are from *Chairil Anwar: Selected Poems,* translated by Burton Raffel and Nurdin Salam (New Directions, 1963).

BURTON RAFFEL

CONTENTS

Introduction   1

Part I
ANGKATAN PUDJANGGA BARU (*The Pudjangga Baru Generation*)

AMIR HAMZAH

Maybe (*Barangkali*)   17
Garden of the World (*Taman Dunia*)   18
There Is Only One (*Hanja Satu*)   19
Smile My Heart, Smile (*Senjum Hatiku, Senjum*)   21
In Praise of You (*Memudji Dikau*)   23
Because of You (*Sebab Dikau*)   24
Opened Blossom (*Terbuka Bunga*)   25
To You, Only You (*Padamu Djua*)   26
Drifting Aloft (*Mengawan*)   28
The Banner in Front of Me (*Pandji Dihadapanku*)   29
Prayer (*Do'a*)   30
Palace of Grace (*Astana Réla*)   31
I'm Drifting (*Hanjut Aku*)   32

SUTAN TAKDIR ALISJAHBANA

Oh Most Beautiful (*Seindah Ini*)   35
Meeting (*Bertemu*)   36
Sacred Fire (*Api Sutji*)   37

AOH KARTAHADIMADJA

Excerpts from *Bits of Diamond* (*Petjahan Ratna*)   40

J. E. TATENGKENG

On the Shore: Twilight (*Dipantai, Waktu Petang*)   46
My Feeling for Art (*Perasaan Seni*)   47
Traveler First Class (*Penumpang Kelas I*)   48

Part II

ANGKATAN '45 (*The Generation of '45*): PIONEERS

CHAIRIL ANWAR

Me (*Aku*)	53
Tuti's Ice Cream (*Tuti Artic*)	54
An Ordinary Song (*Lagu Biasa*)	55
In Vain (*Sia-Sia*)	56
With Patience (*Kesabaran*)	57
Twilight at a Little Harbor (*Sendja di Pelabuhan Ketjil*)	58
Nocturno (*Nocturno*)	59
Love in a Brothel (*title supplied*)	60
My Love Far in the Islands (*Tjintaku Djauh Dipulau*)	61
My Love's on a Far-Away Island (*Tjintaku Djauh Dipulau*)	62
At the Mosque (*Dimesdjid*)	63
To the Painter Affandi (*Kepada Pelukis Affandi*)	64
To a Friend (*Kepada Kawan*)	65
The Captured and the Freed (*Jang Terampas dan Jang Luput*)	66
Annihilation (*Hampa*)	67
Heaven (*Sorga*)	68
A Tale for Dien Tamaela (*Tjerita Buat Dien Tamaela*)	69

RIVAI APIN

Between Two Unfinished Worlds (*Dari Dua Dunia Belum Sudah*)	72
Poems for a Little Sister: IV (*Sadjak Buat Adik: Sadjak IV*)	74
Poems for a Little Sister: VI (*Sadjak Buat Adik: Sadjak VI*)	75
Independence (*Kebebasan*)	76
Son of the Night (*Anak Malam*)	77
Poems for a Little Sister: XIII (*Sadjak Buat Adik: Sadjak XIII*)	79
A Monument (*Tugu*)	80
The Broken Bridge (*Djembatan Patah*)	81
Elegy (*Elegi*)	83

ASRUL SANI

Remember Father, Remember Father (*Kenanglah Bapa,*
   Kenanglah Bapa)   86
A Mother's Letter (*Surat Dari Ibu*)   88

SITI NURAINI

A Woman (*Perempuan*)   90

MOHAMMAD AKBAR DJUHANA

Poète Maudit (*Poète Maudit*)   92

JOKE MOELJONO

She (*Zij*)   94

LOUISE WALUJATI HATMOHARSOIO

Parting (*Berpisah*)   96

Part III
ANGKATAN '45 (*The Generation of '45*): THE LATER IMPULSE

SITOR SITUMORANG

Room No. 2 (*Kamar II: 5 Rue Jouvenet, 4me*)   101
Dawn (*Fadjar*)   102
Thousand Mountain, Jogja (*Gunung Seribu, Jogja*)   103
Sacré Cœur (*Sacré Cœur*)   104
Clear River (*Sungai Bening*)   106
Flowers of Stone (*Bunga Batu*)   107
Quatrain (untitled), in two versions   108
Notes on 1953 (*Tjatatan Tahun 53*)   109
La Ronde: I (*La Ronde: I*)   110
La Ronde: II (*La Ronde: II*)   111
Swimming Pool (*Kolam Berenang*)   112
Morning (*Pagi*)   113
Paris—Avril (*Paris Avril: Jardin des Tuileries*)   114
Pastoral (*Pastoral*)   115
A Woman's Song (*Lagu Perempuan*)   116
Morning Meadow: Sukabumi (*Lapangan Pagi, Sukabumi*)   117

xiii

Visit to a Grave in a Mountain Church (*Ziarah Dalam Geredja Gunung*)   118
Pine Trees and Toadstools (*Tjemara dan Tjendawan*)   119
Waking (*Bangun*)   120
Clock (*Djam*)   121
The Child and Time (*Anak dan Waktu*)   122
M.S. Bali (*M.S. "Bali"*)   123

Toto Sudarto Bachtiar

To a Dead Man (*Kepada Orang Mati*)   126
Night at Sea (*Malam Laut*)   127
Grave (*Kubur*)   128
Nocturno (*Nokturno*)   129
On the Subject of Freedom (*Tentang Kemerdekaan*)   130
Djakarta in the Evening (*Ibukota Sendja*)   131

Samiati Alisjahbana

Quiet Water (*Air Tenang*)   134

Part IV
Angkatan Baru (*The New Generation*)

W. S. Rendra

Ballad of the Killing of Atmo Karpo (*Ballada Terbunuhnja Atmo Karpo*)   139
Kojan the Unfortunate (*Kojan Jang Malang*)   141
Ballad of the Wanderer (*Ballada Petualang*)   142
Ballad of the Men of the Limestone Soil (*Ballada Lelaki-laki Tanah Kapur*)   144
The Proud Child (*Anak Jang Angkuh*)   146
Ballad of the Crucifixion (*Ballada Penjaliban*)   148
Love Letter (*Surat Tjinta*)   150

Ajip Rossidhy

Endai Rasidin's Love Letter (*Surattjinta Endaj Rasidin*)   154

Translators   156

INTRODUCTION

*Thus, modern [Indonesian] literature—the fruit
of dynamic western civilization cutting through
Indonesia's static collectivism—has in the last
forty years been completely detached from traditional Indonesian culture. . . . In spite of the
difference in languages, its fundamental themes
are the same as those of all modern literatures.*

—S. Takdir Alisjahbana, "Le Dévelop-
pement de la langue et de la littérature
indonésiennes," *Cahiers d'Histoire Mon-
diale,* 2:683 (1955)

Indonesia, once the Dutch East Indies, is a tropical country
with about 100,000,000 people and 3,000 miles of very beautiful, mostly very fertile islands (Sumatra, Java, Bali, and
hundreds more). It has produced a rich, varied, and ancient
literature; yet the Indonesian literature in this book is only
three or four decades old. What looks like a minor paradox
melts in your hands. The ancient literature was composed
not in any one, uniform national language but in Javanese,
in Sundanese, in Minangkabau—in short, in certain of the
approximately two hundred regional tongues which have
family resemblances to *bahasa Indonesia,* now the Indonesian national language, yet cannot be understood by those
who speak only *bahasa Indonesia.* Nor can those who speak,
say, Javanese, understand someone speaking only Minangkabau: these are not simply dialects but fully separate
tongues. (Other languages in the same large Malayo-Polyne-
sian family are spoken on Taiwan, in the Philippines, in
Hawaii, and all the way across to Madagascar.)

This new Indonesian literature matured with astonishing
quickness: I want to say a few brief things about its new
language, and about the literary situation which emerged
along with it. Conceding the "detachment" of Indonesian
literature from its ancient predecessors, I also want to indi-
cate at least the major influences out of the past and point

1

out, too, those marks of "dynamic western civilization" which are clearly central to the developing new tradition. Finally, I want to explore some of the chief paths already taken by Indonesian poetry, and particularly the rough boundaries of its achievement.

Bahasa Indonesia received its name, and began to be accepted as a national tongue, only in the 1920's; there were stirrings as early as 1922, when Muhammad Yamin brought out a volume of untraditional Malay verse. It was based, in part, on bazaar Malay, *Melaju pasar*, the old *lingua franca* both of the Dutch East Indies and of the many principalities and kingdoms that preceded European colonialization; *Melaju pasar* was leavened with the purer, more highly developed Malay used on Sumatra (the primal home of the language). Dutch colonial administrators gave Malay a kind of inter-island status, frequently using it as a "native" language, in preference to their own "civilized" one, when dealing with their brown-skinned subjects. Indonesians had been obliged to use Malay among themselves when no regional language existed in common; they made a virtue of necessity and adopted this *bahasa Melaju*, now renamed *bahasa Indonesia*, as a part of their nationalist cause. Indeed, the newly named, newly accepted national language became another rallying point for growing nationalist aspirations.

Although the new Indonesian language was at first the maternal tongue of very few Indonesians, its closeness to the regional languages, as well as the intensity of Indonesian national aspirations and the linguistic talents and sophistication of the incredibly multilingual Indonesian people, made it almost inevitable that literary activity in *bahasa Indonesia* begin at once. Amir Hamzah's magnificent *Njanji Sunji* (Songs of Loneliness) appeared in 1935, and the poems had already appeared, individually, in *Pudjangga Baru* (The New Writer)—but of this, more in a moment.

The language comes from Malay, but for the most part the literature does not. It should be remembered, too, that the Malay language was born in Sumatra, an Indonesian island, and not in Malaya proper—and, in any case, that there are perhaps four million Malays in Malaysia, but

2

100,000,000 Indonesians. One of the rare Malay progenitors of modern Indonesian verse is Hamzah Pansuri (or Fansjuri) of Barus in Sumatra, a sixteenth- and seventeenth-century metaphysical poet:

> Satukan hangat dan dingin,
> Tinggalkan loba dan ingin,
> Hanchor hendak saperti lilin,
> Mangka-nya dapat kerja-mu lichin.

> When hot and cold combine,
> When greed and desire have faded out,
> When all wanting melts like wax,
> Then your road will be like glass, like smooth stone.

Hamzah Pansuri is worth attention for two reasons. As R. O. Winstedt has said, "For the student of poetry his metaphysical verse makes him incomparably the greatest literary figure among religious writers in the Malay language." Winstedt adds: "A religious writer who could adapt the metre of the *sha'ir* and the figures and phrases of the *pantun* to the expression of the erotic mysticism of the Persian poets is a unique figure and struck a new note in Malay literature" (*A History of Malay Literature*, 1940, pp. 93, 96). In short, he was a poet who worked with indigenous forms and traditions, making such "vulgar" vehicles carry more exalted messages than writers before him had thought possible. In particular, though he used the verse form known as *sjair* (or *sha'ir*), he also drew upon perhaps the most exciting of all Malay/Indonesian indigenous forms, the *pantun*—a four-line, closely rhymed little poem, divided into two self-contained and often very different couplets, and capable of concisely, flavorfully expressing emotions ranging far wider than the end-stopped couplet can carry in English. (Winstedt, p. 129, observes that "as his editor Dr. Doorenbos has noticed, Hamzah's poetry is full of tags from the *pantun*.") A *pantun*'s first couplet is usually bold and sweeping; the second couplet shifts the focus to some more specific, more personal image, related to that introduced in the first lines, but subtly, often very subtly:

3

Kerengga di-dalam buloh,
Serahi berisi ayer mawar:
Sampai hasrat di-dalam tuboh,
Tuan sa-orang jadi penawar.

Big red ants are in the bamboo,
The flask is filled with rose water:
When there's desire in my body
Only one man can cure me.

One reason the *pantun* is still popular today, I suspect, is its easy convertibility to whatever subject happens to be on one's mind. Romance is the most common theme, but the wise grumbling of peasant-farmers finds just as suitable expression:

Bukan tanah mendjadi padi,
Kalau djadi, hampa melajang.
Bukan bangsa mendjadi hadji,
Djadi hadji tak pernah sembahjang.

This soil is no good for rice,
But if it grows, the wind will blow it away.
He's not the kind of man who should be a *hadji*,
Because now that he's a *hadji* he never prays.

Rice is, of course, the national food, and a national preoccupation of Indonesians. A *hadji* is one who has fulfilled a prime religious duty, and in lay eyes attained holiness, by making the prescribed pilgrimage to Mecca—and only the comparatively wealthy can afford it. The poor worker in the rice paddies cannot hope to become a *hadji*, but he knows good soil from bad, and good men from the shallow sort on whom holy titles sit like just another hat. It is suggested, too, that a poor man's piety may plant deeper roots, may resist the wind, even though he will never attain exalted rank or travel the formal pathways of organized holiness.

The earliest Malays probably emigrated, some two or three thousand years B.C., from Yunnan province, China. (See "Origin, Migrations and Language," the second chapter of Winstedt's *The Malays, A Cultural History*, 5th ed., 1958.) One final *pantun*, in Derwent May's translation, illustrates, I think, something of the distant but archaeologically proved racial and cultural kinship; readers of Ar-

4

thur Waley's Chinese translations should feel immediate similarities:

Pulau Pandan djauh ditengah
Dibalik Pulau Angsa Dua
Hantjur badan dikandung tanah
Budi baik terkenang djua

Out in the sea the island of pines,
Behind it the isle of the two geese:
Let my body be ruined, buried in the earth,
His kind ways will not be forgotten.

The *pantun* has been a potent influence, and in the early days of the 1920's and 1930's a very direct influence, on modern Indonesian poetry. Less direct, but perhaps equally pervasive, has been the effect of another indigenous expression, the Malay/Indonesian proverb. The proverb need not rhyme, although significantly it sometimes does. But the good proverb must carry that sharp, frequently amazingly deft and brief thrust which also distinguishes the best of modern Indonesian verse.

Laksana buah kedempong,
Luar berisi, dalam kosong.

Like wormy fruit,
Firm on the outside, empty within.

Pantas
Tewas.

The smart-aleck
Gets it in the neck.

Kera lotong terlalu makan,
Tupai didjulai timpa perasan.

If the monkeys in the tree-tops eat too much
The squirrels down below are drowned in the taste.

When Sutan Takdir Alisjahbana, Amir Hamzah, and Armijn Pane founded *Pudjangga Baru* (The New Writer) in 1933, they were joint enterprisers on very new seas. There had never been a publication written exclusively in the new national language, *bahasa Indonesia*, and devoting itself exclusively to Indonesian life and letters. There had never been a publication edited exclusively by Indonesians—not

5

really surprising, since in 1938–39, with a population of about 72,000,000, only 204 Indonesians were permitted to graduate from high school. It did not matter that *Pudjangga Baru*'s circulation was tiny. By printing, and fervently encouraging an outpouring of romantic, humanitarian poems, stories, and articles, by discussing cultural problems that the Dutch did not see as quite so seditious as in fact they were, *Pudjangga Baru* was midwife to a literary revolution. The political revolution followed not long after: if the connection is not a causative one, neither is the sequence accidental.

> Solitude floats on the still air,
> While the palm trees in the courtyard throw long shadows,
> Expanding but vague,
> Spilling over feeling—oh, flooding memory . . .
> —J. E. TATENGKENG, *Petang* (Twilight)

Tatengkeng's "expanding but vague" romanticism neatly summarizes the mood of the day: yearning, almost desperate to catch up to the rest of the world, to achieve national fulfillment. It did not matter, either, that this yearning mood had no very clear focus. What *Pudjangga Baru* did not supply, or was prevented from supplying by the restrictions of a watchful colonial government, was fairly easily filled in by a people being swept out of "static collectivism," by a people confronted in day-to-day living with the techniques and the theories of western civilization, with the history of bold political manifestoes, with brilliant sanitary and medical and scientific achievements of all kinds, with machines and weapons and a host of art forms all of which were aglow with the shiny reflection of western might. No wonder, to cite again the testimony of Takdir Alisjahbana, that "these intellectuals no longer felt at home in their families and home villages. For them the sacred old tradition no longer had the same meaning it had had for their parents. They criticized the old standards, the old ways and ideas; this is why the new literature, understood broadly, was above all else dedicated to social polemic" (1955).

Amir Hamzah, the greatest poet of the *Pudjangga Baru* group, experienced this conflict in the most direct fashion. His family forced him to renounce the girl he loved, and

6

marry instead one chosen by them. Hamzah's two volumes of verse, *Njanji Sunji* (Songs of Loneliness) and *Buah Rindu* (Fruits of Longing), unite fervent Islamic mysticism with the yearning and bottled-up desire typical of his generation. The tension between God as beloved and the mortal beloved is basic to his work:

> I am bewildered, half mad,
> But my love keeps coming to You;
> You suck in my desire
> Like a girl hiding behind a curtain. . . .
> *(Padamu Djua, To You, Only You)*

> . . . When the covering is peeled away,
> When all mists are pushed to the side,
> Light will leap and sparkle deep inside us
> And a holy brightness of desire will gush out.
> *(Pandji Dihadapanku, The Banner in Front of Me)*

Even Takdir Alisjahbana, profoundly western, philosopher, grammarian, and lexicographer as well as novelist and poet, shared and gave poignant expression to his generation's ambivalence:

> While my breath swells
> And my heart beats
> Oh fire, grill my soul
> Till it screams, till it sighs. . . .

> So God's mercy pours steadily forth,
> So the pleasant fire scorches;
> The song is only my anguished cries.
> *(Api Sutji, Sacred Fire)*

The Japanese invasion and occupation of Indonesia enormously accelerated processes both political and literary. By crushing the Dutch and by replacing strict paternal western administrators with at least a certain number of Indonesian governors, the Japanese ensured the finality of the national revolution. Literature went underground from 1942 to 1945, but the ferment that had been relatively private and limited, before the war, became almost a universal phenomenon. People met in small groups; poems and other writings were circulated in manuscript; and a whole new generation swept

7

into being, the so-called Generation of '45, *Angkatan '45.*
"The difference between the Pudjangga Baru generation
and the post-war generation is lessened reliance on [mere]
rhetoric. . . . The Pudjangga Baru group's nationalism
was something new-born, seen, often, through rose-colored
glasses and all felt in exaggerated terms. The post-war generation's . . . chief slogan was: Everything completely
new" (H. B. Jassin, *Gema Tanah Air*, Echoes of Our Country, p. 5).

The primal figure in this "completely new" literary movement was unquestionably Chairil Anwar, a savagely brilliant, hard-living, hard-drinking, cynical, romantic, fiercely
Indonesian poet who in a brief lifetime and with a total output of fewer than seventy-five original poems transformed
the poetic scene. Dead at the age of twenty-seven, Anwar
had fully absorbed the new directions taken by European
and American writing; indeed, he translated from Heming-
way, from Rilke's letters and poetry, and from the poetry
of T. S. Eliot, Conrad Aiken, and the Dutch writer Du Per-
ron, besides adapting and imitating work by Archibald Mac-
Leish, Lorca, and the Dutchmen Marsman and Slauerhoff.

> When my time comes
> I want to hear no one's cries,
> Nor yours either . .
> (*Aku*, Me)

Aku ends, defiant, unhopeful, but in no way resigned, with
the exultant cry: "I want to live a thousand years."

The breaking down of prewar colonial society broke
down, for Chairil, all conventions: when he addresses President Soekarno, the George Washington of Indonesia, his
tone is irreverently familiar:

Hey! Friend Soekarno, give me your hand and let's set everything
  ship-shape. . . .
You and me, we're made out of the same stuff, we've got the same
  veins . . .
  (*Persetudjuan Dengan Bung Karno*, Agreement with Friend
  Soekarno)

Even with God his tone is unrestrained:

8

I shouted at Him
Until He came . . .
(*Dimesdjid*, At the Mosque)

His bluntness can stab and caress at the same time, as in this
four-line poem, untitled in the original. I have called it
"Your Mouth":

Your mouth was biting at mine
In that moment hatred boiled up in me
Why didn't I strangle you
While you were gently hurting me??

He was also aware of traditional forms and, when he used
them, brilliantly transformed them:

I am Pattiradjawane
Whom the gods watch over
I alone.

I am Pattiradjawane,
Foam of the sea.
The sea is my blood. . . .
(*Tjerita Buat Dien Tamaela*, A Tale for
Dien Tamaela)

Anwar can be bitterly wistful:

. . . I am like you, everything ran by,
Me and Tuti and Greet and Amoi . . .
Dilapidated hearts.
Love's a danger that quickly fades.
(*Tuti Artic*, Tuti's Ice Cream)

He can be unabashedly tender:

Our garden
doesn't spread out very far, it's a little affair
in which we won't lose each other.
For you and me it's enough. . . .
(*Taman*, Our Garden)

He can be wryly, knowingly mocking and at the same time
understanding, managing to disentangle himself even as he
admits kinship with what he is leaving forever behind:

Like my mother, and my grandmother too,
Plus seven generations before them,
I also seek admission to heaven,

9

Which the Moslem Party and the Mohammedan Party say has rivers of milk
And thousands of houris all over. . . .
    (*Sorga*, Heaven)

Anwar is by any standard a major poet, comparable, in my opinion, with the first-rate in any language, East or West. He and his generation, the *Angkatan '45*, had ". . . discovered hope/All of it in one Word and because of one Word"—the lines are from Rivai Apin's *Dari Dua Dunia Belum Sudah* (Between Two Unfinished Worlds), and the Word is *Merdeka*, "freedom." They had also discovered Blake's "invisible worm/That flies in the night," and they poured their jarring new insights into new forms, new sounds. The measure of the change they effected can perhaps be gauged by quoting from the postwar work of J. E. Tatengkeng, a charter member of the *Pudjangga Baru* group, from whose earlier "Twilight" I have already given an excerpt.

> Before I was thirty
> I was never more than a deck passenger.
> Thanks to the efforts of my friends
> And the transfer of sovereignty
> I'm now a traveler first class. . . .
>   (*Penumpang Kelas I*, Traveler First Class)

This kind of spare, hard verse is in a sense the touchstone of modern Indonesian poetry. "Rose-colored" glasses are no longer permissible: the problem is how to move on, how to take Anwar's new frontier as a starting point for further advances. Two poets in particular, Sitor Situmorang and the very young W. S. Rendra, seem to me to have been most successful at this task.

The closest to Chairil Anwar, and like him a member of the *Angkatan '45*, is Sitor Situmorang. Born in 1924, or two years after Chairil Anwar, and for some years resident in Paris, Sitor has much of Anwar's sharp-etched, western-toned imagery, and much the same distrust of easy solutions. He is more explicitly intellectual; he is often a good deal more erotic.

Long before morning the sky splits,
The party is over. Only a pool
Of spilled wine is left, like blood.
The morning is red and festering. . . .
   (*Pagi*, Morning)

. . . Lying on the evening's breast. "You're all mine,"
Moaning seconds flow into kisses,
Angry lips grope for time
To squeeze it into the body of a woman. . . .
   (*La Ronde: I*)

Sitor's political concern, easily understandable in any member of the Generation of '45, may have affected his poetry. But he has already deepened and widened the road Chairil Anwar opened, made it less stark and perhaps more consciously mature. Toto Sudarto Bachtiar—a young poet whose great gift is lyric—carries this process one stage farther; I suspect that without Sitor's prior "mediation" it might not have been possible to turn Chairil's influence so readily into such different channels.

W. S. Rendra, born in 1935, is a wizard. I am not now going to quote from any of his poems, which are well represented toward the end of this book. Rendra's verse is cumulative, accelerating, and too tightly spun for excerpts to reflect accurately what he has done. His method is dangerous, clearly, since it depends to a very high degree on long-limbed and sometimes rather rhetorical phrases. His 1957 collection is significantly entitled *Ballada Orang-Orang Tertjinta* (Lovers' Ballads, or Ballads of Those Who Are Beloved). It contains none of the swift, short capsules hurled onto the page by Chairil Anwar (and to a somewhat lesser degree by Sitor Situmorang). The shortest poem in the Rendra volume has twenty lines, and some are much longer. Aside from *Tjerita Buat Dien Tamaela*, noted earlier, there is only one poem of more than twenty lines in Chairil Anwar's principal collection, *Deru Tjampur Debu* (Noise Mixed with Dust). Rendra's excitement and power, his new rhythms and even newer tonalities, make him, in my judgment, potentially the most impressive and galvanizing influence to appear on the Indonesian poetic scene since Anwar himself. (Rendra's glowing religious feeling, and what Derwent May has called "that extraordinary generous and gentle humanity of his," need no more introduction than a reading of his poems.)

And then there are the others, from all the generations, still active, newly active. Poetry is wholly alive in Indonesia: a book this size, dealing with a literature so rich, cannot hope to do justice anywhere. I plead guilty to overstressing A, omitting B, and choosing all the wrong poems by C. But my basic aim in selecting the poems and poets represented has been to include only the first-rate, and by that I mean poetry which is first-rate in English as well as in Indonesian. (The roughly chronological arrangement of the poets is a matter of convenience only, and I can assure those unfamiliar with Indonesian poetry that the chronology is very rough indeed.) This is a book meant to be read in English, and as English: although I have striven to let Indonesian poets speak in as many different voices as I could persuade into this project, nothing has been included for any reason but the excellence of its translated version.

I want to say about Indonesian prosody, here, only that *bahasa Indonesia* is rhyme-rich and that the poets are aware of the fact. No rhymes have been translated: Indonesian poetry is so entirely different from that in English, in sound, syntax, and almost every other linguistic category, that a translation, if it succeeds, is necessarily a complete transmutation. Nor are the forms employed sufficiently helpful to an understanding and appreciation of the poetry to merit discussion in a general work of this sort.

Let these multiple voices sing however loud and clear they are able, with no further mediation.

Note: Each of the brief biographical introductions to individual poets is followed by a list of books of poetry published by that poet. These lists are not intended to furnish a complete bibliography.

Part I

ANGKATAN PUDJANGGA BARU

The Pudjangga Baru Generation

Amir Hamzah

BORN on February 28, 1911, in Sumatra, Hamzah died in March, 1946, in what is usually called the "social revolution." (W. F. Wertheim, *Indonesian Society in Transition*, p. 160, speaks of "a brutal massacre of many of the local aristocratic leaders and their families . . . murdered to the last male descendant.") Well educated, nephew of a sultan, one of the central experiences of Hamzah's life was his intense love affair with a girl considered unsuitable by his family. He did not marry her—was obliged not to marry her—and the scars never left him. The brief inscription at the end of *Njanji Sunji* (Songs of Loneliness), his most famous volume of poetry, is autobiographically accurate:

> A flower floating in a loose knot of hair
> Gave birth to my sorrowful poems.

Deeply committed to Islam, Hamzah centers much of his poetry on the ambiguity (and tension) between God as beloved and the other beloved, the mortal beloved he was not permitted to have. Other important influences include a deep knowledge of and fondness for classical Malay culture (both literary and linguistic) and a sensitive awareness of Persian and other oriental literatures. Hamzah translated the Bhagavad Gita and edited *Setanggi Timur* (Incense from the East), containing poems translated from the Persian, Chinese, Hindi, Japanese, and Turkish. His brother, Amal Hamzah, translated Rabindranath Tagore's *Gitanjali*.

Hamzah's poetry offers few formal innovations; indeed, his use of traditional Malay locutions sometimes makes him difficult reading. James S Holmes ("A Quarter Century of Indonesian Literature," *Books Abroad*, 1955) observes that "though they were often archaic in language even when they were written . . . [his poems] remain the finest produced before the war, and the last pure flowering of traditional Malay." The force and sometimes incredible intensity

15

which Hamzah expresses in these essentially orthodox words and patterns make his work one of the chief touchstones for Indonesian poetry.

Njanji Sunji (Songs of Loneliness), 1935; *Buah Rindu* (Fruits of Longing), 1941; (ed.) *Setanggi Timur* (Incense from the East), 1939.

MAYBE

Barangkali

You who lie quietly in my heart
Like the thinnest breath of heaven,
Enfolding the world in your immensity,
Yet so small an eyebrow hides you,

I raise you up,
My tongue exalts you,
I wrap you in my song,
Rock you in my lullabies.

Up, oh Mountain,
Open your eye of pearl,
Move your delicate fingers
Along the strings of the lute of Paradise—

Let the goddess of song awaken,
Love's dancer, slender and straight,
Supple as leaping fire,
Subtle as incense.

Dance, virgin, dance,
Sing in your golden voice:
Maybe the waves of memory will break,
Will crash, will lie dead on the shore of my heart.

TRANSLATED BY S. T. ALISJAHBANA, SABINA THORNTON,
AND BURTON RAFFEL

GARDEN OF THE WORLD

Taman Dunia

You take me into the garden of the world, my darling!
You guide my fingers, point to the laughing flowers and the
half-ripened smiling blossoms.
You bend my stiff head to kiss the lonely, hidden, sweet-
smelling scent.
You stroke my longing cheek, gently, softly, with the velvet
leaves.
I am surprised, astonished, struck dumb.
You whisper:
"Garden of Paradise, Garden of Paradise
Made like mother-of-pearl."
Then you disappear.
I am as dazed as a madman.

TRANSLATED BY BURTON RAFFEL AND NURDIN SALAM

THERE IS ONLY ONE

Hanja Satu

Your heart shapes a thought:
Rain falls, a storm beats down,
And Your garden is smashed,
Is broken and drowned.

Tiny men run every which way,
Slipping, falling;
The water keeps on rising,
Old trees come crashing to the ground.

Shouting and screaming hang muffled
In the thunder's roll.
Lightning spits through the darkness,
A tongue of fire shoots straight up.

The covered ark floats quietly on the water,
Sheltering Noah Your belovèd,
Free,
A peaceful voice in a world full of fear.

*   *   *

Grace guards the shepherd's head,
Old Abraham's beautiful children,
Born—like the light from different diamonds—
To different mothers.

Now we quarrel
About which is really the precious stone:
The great jewelers of all the centuries
Never bothered to leave an appraisal.

Hamzah   19

But ah, my belovèd,
What good is all this to me?
There is only One I wait for, longing
To feel You as close
As Moses on the heights of Sinai.

TRANSLATED BY S. T. ALISJAHBANA, SABINA THORNTON,
AND BURTON RAFFEL

Hamzah

SMILE MY HEART, SMILE

Senjum Hatiku, Senjum

Smile my heart, smile.
Laugh my heart, laugh.
Your sorrow, my friend, oh keep it down
Though your heart is sure it will crack.

In fact, the roses have bloomed,
The jasmine flowers have opened out their buds,
There are girls sitting and singing with happiness,
But you, ah beggar, you're simply ignored.

I know doves go feeding each other,
Magpies chatter, singing of love,
But you, oh stranger,
You're like an owl moping for the moon.

Indeed, the ocean embraces the sun,
The moon is encircled by stars,
But you, ah wanderer,
Who will caress your anxious heart?

Be quiet, my heart, be quiet.
Try to be gay, my heart, try to be gay.
Your sorrow, my friend, try to bury it
The way bark will bury a fire.

Who let the butterflies go playing—
Let the waves sniff at the shore—
While I, the noblest creature God made,
Wear love and sorrow around my head?

Hamzah   21

Be still, my heart, be still.
Why worry, whatever happens?
This is only the way things run on
When your Mother lets you sit on her lap.

TRANSLATED BY BURTON RAFFEL AND NURDIN SALAM

Hamzah

IN PRAISE OF YOU

Memudji Dikau

When I praise You, with closed lips, my eyes shut,
I bow down on my knees, my head on the ground, deep in
   silence, in the darkness of Supreme Love.
Your belovèd comes to me, finds me sitting alone, lonely
   and quiet.
She kisses my lips, clings to my shoulders, hangs on my neck,
   desiring only the sound of love.
While my heart sings, and my whole body bends in prayer,
   she presses my thighs, drinking my voice . . .
And
She floats back to her home,
Pure light,
A tongue of fire wrapped in glass,
Ascending toward grace, and the blessing of peace.

TRANSLATED BY BURTON RAFFEL AND NURDIN SALAM

BECAUSE OF YOU

Sebab Dikau

Flowers burst into bloom,
Loving life because of You:
Love spreading like flowers in my heart
Filled it with the fragrance of blossoms, and their dust.

Life is a dream, something
Played behind a screen, and I,
Now dreamer, now dancer, am pulled
In and out of existence.

So the bright leather puppet shines
His shadow on the screen, bringing us a world
Of emotions. The longing heart follows;
Two souls join, fuse.

I am a puppet, you are a puppet,
To please the puppeteer as he runs through his song;
We glance at each other, out on the open screen,
For as long as the one melody lasts.

Other bright-colored dolls take their turn;
You and I are laid in our box.
I am a puppet, you are a puppet,
To please the puppeteer running out his rhymes.

TRANSLATED BY S. T. ALISJAHBANA, SABINA THORNTON,
AND BURTON RAFFEL

OPENED BLOSSOM

Terbuka Bunga

A flower unfolds in my heart!
A leafy blossom touched by your fragrant lips,
Bending to watch your smile of grace and blessing.
As this flower opens
Those that came before it wither and fade, my darling.
This is the flower of my heart; in the time when I was a
    wanderer it symbolized you.
Belovèd! Is this truly the flower that can never fade?

TRANSLATED BY BURTON RAFFEL AND NURDIN SALAM

Hamzah   25

TO YOU, ONLY YOU

Padamu Djua

My love is scraped
Away, evaporated,
And I return again
To You.

You burn like a lantern in the darkness,
Set in a window
To call me slowly back,
And patient, faithful forever.

My Belovèd is One:
But I am mortal,
Longing to touch,
Longing to see,

And You,
Invisible,
Your voice blurred,
Hold my heart only with words;

You are jealous,
Cruel,
Dangling me helpless in Your claws,
First free, then snatched up again.

I am bewildered, half mad,
But my love keeps coming to You;
You suck in my desire
Like a girl hiding behind a curtain.

Hamzah

Your love is lonely
And waits alone.
Time passes—it's not my turn;
The day dies—but not my friend . . .

TRANSLATED BY S. T. ALISJAHBANA, SABINA THORNTON,
AND BURTON RAFFEL

DRIFTING ALOFT

Mengawan

I pull away from myself; following my guard I go floating up.
Down there I see, stretched out, limp and feeble, me, dirty,
　　uncared-for, four unities united in one.
Thoughts come, spreading memory, brightening the past
　　with a bold, shining light, turning as clear as a mirror.
They go slowly by me, and by her, gaily laughing, sadly
　　happy, poignantly in love, like pigeons mouth to mouth.
My soul smiles with pity.
A thing longing for a thing . . .
I go drifting up, mercifully, following my guard carrying the
　　news.
Be strong, my powerful wings, carry me, let me come to
　　where, no matter how lightly, I can reach out and caress
　　that musky chair.

TRANSLATED BY BURTON RAFFEL AND NURDIN SALAM

　　　　　　　　　　　　　　　　　　　　　　　　Hamzah

THE BANNER IN FRONT OF ME

Pandji Dihadapanku

You wave a banner in front of me,
Bright green, hung on a pole of pearls.
You walk at my right, a slow escort, calm, eternally just, each
of us young, each of us innocent and flooded with a
perfect affection.
In the darkness there are four of us eagerly waiting, listening
for that gentle voice, that drawn-out call, fading, drifting
away.
In the darkness there are four of us, begging, pleading for
the misty screen to open, the fine-spun wrapping around
the most important point of all:
When the covering is peeled away,
When all mists are pushed to the side,
Light will leap and sparkle deep inside us
And a holy brightness of desire will gush out.

TRANSLATED BY BURTON RAFFEL AND NURDIN SALAM

PRAYER

Do'a

With what do I compare our meeting, my darling?

With the vague soft dusk, when the full moon rises, having
driven off the weary, blazing heat.

With the sweetness of the evening wind, cooling the body,
floating the senses, bearing reflection, sweeping illusions
in under your chair.

My heart brightens, hearing you, like stars setting out their
candles.

My soul opens, awaiting your love, as the night-blooming
jasmine unfolds its petals.

Oh, darling, fill my heart with your voice, fill my breast with
your glow,
Let my dimmed eyes shine, my sad laugh brighten!

TRANSLATED BY BURTON RAFFEL AND NURDIN SALAM

PALACE OF GRACE

Astana Réla

We will not have each other, in this world;
My love, do not be sad.
The world will not be our home forever,
Let your thoughts soar to the clouds.

Do not believe their scornful whispers:
It is not only for the world to say.
Use your own eyes, your own mind,
And humble your heart before Him.

In the beginning there was nothing,
We met in time's midst;
At the third moment we shall leave them all
And face each other, in the brightness of the End.

If your Belovèd longs for you,
And I am in the lap of His grace,
Then will be the time for us
To see our happiness reflected in the moving waters:

We shall harvest the fruit together,
The blessing of our work on the face of the earth.
Flowering scorn will fade and wither.
Only happiness will smile its fragrant smile.

And there, for the first time,
We will feel together, together read
The bright inscription worked with pearls
On the great gate of the Palace of Grace.

TRANSLATED BY S. T. ALISJAHBANA, SABINA THORNTON,
AND BURTON RAFFEL

I'M DRIFTING

Hanjut Aku

I'm drifting, my darling,
Drifting away!
Reach out your hand, help me.
I'm surrounded by a desert silence!
There is no loving voice, no wind to cool my heart, no water
    for my thirst,
My thirst for your love, my yearning for your whisper.
I will die of your silence.
The sky covers me like a web, the water lies still,
And I am sinking,
Sinking into the night.
The water above me presses down, down,
The earth below rejects me.
I am dead, my darling, I am dead!

TRANSLATED BY BURTON RAFFEL AND NURDIN SALAM

Hamzah

Sutan Takdir Alisjahbana

BORN on February 11, 1908, in Sumatra, Alisjahbana studied law, linguistics, literature, and philosophy, and was for a time a teacher in Palembang, Sumatra. His long association with the publishing organization Balai Pustaka (Government Publishing House—so-called after 1928, having been founded in 1918 as Commissie voor de Volkslectuur, or Bureau for Popular Literature) began in 1930. Balai Pustaka published his first novel, *Tak Putus Dirundung Malang* (Misfortune without End), in 1929, and the three later novels that appeared in 1932, 1936, and 1941. *Pudjangga Baru* (The New Writer), an extremely influential journal founded and edited by Alisjahbana, Amir Hamzah, and Armijn Pane, printed some of the best work of the best prewar writers, including Amir Hamzah, Armijn and Sanoesi Pane, J. E. Tatengkeng, and Alisjahbana himself. *Pudjangga Baru* was first published in 1933; suspended in 1942, it resumed in 1948; in 1953 it was replaced by *Konfrontasi* (Confrontation), again edited by Alisjahbana.

In many respects the dean of Indonesian letters, Alisjahbana is not simply a literary figure. In 1943, under the Japanese occupation, he became secretary of the Komisi Bahasa Indonesia (Indonesian Language Commission), charged with updating *bahasa Indonesia*; from 1946 to 1948 he was a professor of the Indonesian language at the National University, Djakarta. He has published widely on linguistic matters, including a well-known *Tatabahasa Baru Bahasa Indonesia* (A New Grammar of the Indonesian Language). Since the war, too, he has interested himself in cultural and philosophic problems, participating in a number of international conferences; in 1959–60 he was in residence at the Institute for Advanced Research in the Social Sciences, California. In 1950 he published *Soal Kebudajaan Indonesia Di-tengah-tengah Dunia* (Indonesia's Cultural Problems in Today's World).

Alisjahbana, an important literary figure, is not a poetic figure of the same stature as Amir Hamzah. Always deeply concerned with *masjarakat Indonesia*, the Indonesian community as a whole, his verse expresses an essentially thoughtful, sensitive approach to existence and some of its central problems. *Bertemu* (Meeting), included here, was written after the death of his first wife.

Tebaran Mega (Scattered Clouds), 1936.

OH MOST BEAUTIFUL

Seindah Ini

God,
Do you hear the bird's song at twilight,
Mourning the day in the lonely woods?
I felt myself crushed, watching your light
Trailing across the hill,
Slowly becoming evening and invisible.

Oh heart, cry, cry!
How pleasant and skillful are your tears.
And why resist, oppose?
Thank you, God, for this heart
So sincere, so susceptible, so full of beauty,
This heart that weeps with sharp pain,
When weeping,
That laughs with bright joy,
When laughing,
That loves flamingly,
When in love,
And fights with fierce courage,
In war.

TRANSLATED BY BURTON RAFFEL AND NURDIN SALAM

MEETING

Bertemu

Standing beside the grave
With the morning sun glistening pink on the earth,
My soul bends down
Seeking your face,
And my senses swell and flood.

Confronting you,
Piercing the thick ground,
I let my eyes wander
To the rows of graves, hundreds of stones
In red earth, in thick grass,
Mossy wood and singing marble,

And like lightning it flashed in my heart:
So many sorrows well up,
So often sadness slices tears
Onto the earth.
Oh, my sister in white,
You're not alone in the ground!

And my poor soul bends
To the feet of the One God:
Before Him my sorrows are the world's sorrows
My misery the world's misery.
I am dust in the air,
Blown by the wind.
A cool dew drops on my soul
And shines brightly in my eyes.

TRANSLATED BY BURTON RAFFEL AND NURDIN SALAM

Alisjahbana

SACRED FIRE

Api Sutji

While my breath swells
And my heart beats
Oh fire, grill my soul
Till it screams, till it sighs.

Like glowing steel
Kindled in bright flames
Let my soul melt
In the Supreme One's blaze.

I feel a tightness press on my heart,
My eyes are nervous and wild,
In my quiet seat I am pursued.

So God's mercy pours steadily forth,
So the pleasant fire scorches;
The song is only my anguished cries.

TRANSLATED BY BURTON RAFFEL AND NURDIN SALAM

Aoh Kartahadimadja

Born September 15, 1911, in Bandung, Java, Kartaha-dimadja graduated from the Dutch middle school (MULO). Until late in 1939 he was employed on a tea plantation, but a serious illness in 1940 and a five-month convalescence gave him both the time to read and an interest in literature. S. T. Alisjahbana, *Puisi Baru* (The New Poetry), records that he was "especially attracted by Norwegian writers."

During the Japanese occupation, Kartahadimadja served as a translator with the Kantor Pusat Kebudajaan (Central Cultural Office). Simultaneously he was secretary of Ang-katan Baru (The New Generation), a society of young artists, and active on the editorial committee of the Java-nese Dramatic Society. He later went to Europe, working for Radio Hilversum (Holland), then for the Translation Bureau of Sticusa, a Dutch intercultural organization. He is now employed by the B.B.C., London.

Kartahadimadja is a religious and very specifically an Islamic poet. Writing sometimes in traditional verse forms, sometimes in prose poem style (as did Amir Hamzah), he is not in any way an innovator. As Bakri Siregar notes, in his *Penjair dan Sandjak* (Poets and Poems, p. 74), "One is more likely to place his poetry with that of *Pudjangga Baru*, though his later output could be classified in the Gen-eration of '45." At his worst inclined to sentimentality, at his best he breathes a clear, warm new life into outwardly unadventuresome lines.

Zahra (two cycles of poetry and "Lakbok," a play in three acts), 1950.

Excerpts from BITS OF DIAMOND

Petjahan Ratna

II

Do you know, oh little sister, the lightning's flash, God's love for you?

The clouds break apart, I stand up, I paddle the little boat again.

And though I smash against the surf and the rocks, I'll still be happy, knowing my bones are scattered across the bottom of the ocean, together with pearls that remember you!

III

Like the dark curving sky, heavy with scattered stars, oh my darling, so richly soft is your veiled hair.

Your hooded black hair, curling, spread with blue silk flowers, oh beauty, the pen breaks, there are no words.

Only memory covers over the dusk, the sun goes down, you leave me . . .

IV

It can't be long before I close my eyes forever . . .

I'm ready! I can see us, you and me, riding in a golden hearse, pulled by horses dancing with joy.

The cheering bystanders play all sorts of noisy instruments, we pass the gate all hung with flowers and waving banners.

I'm ready, I'll be the first to go . . .

V

Are you surprised, little one, that I still skip and dance, still sing cheerfully, knowing my tree will bear no fruit?

Ah, why not?

The trees, the birds, the rivers sing, why shouldn't I join in?

Kartahadimadja

Trees rustle gently in the dry season's choking heat. Birds sing in the broken branches. The pure waterfall booms down into the valley below.

Why shouldn't I sing, too, in my dry season that lasts all the year through, sing from the parched, cracked branches, alongside the valley as dark as night?

VI

My heart beats like thunder:
There's an unexpected letter,
Written in the coils and loops of a strange hand,
Strange for this whole last year.

If it's true I can't have what I want
I will have no descendants
And my name will be clearly,
Beautifully carved into the coral rock—

With a painful smile
Chiselled into the stone,
To stand in bold relief, keeping off misfortune:
"Not cracked by the heat, not rotted by the rain."

X

You made the flowers in their whirling color,
You made the sun glow and the earth bright, oh my God, and for all of us.

Why is Your love so great, showering such infinite grace upon us?

Flowers wear drops of jewels to welcome the dawn, the streams of reddish clouds cry and shout, and I cannot look away.

Why did You also fill my heart with songs of swelling desire, of love and praise?

XIII

In my tiny, carved box I set aside your letters as soft and fine as silk.

When the ink flows no more, when the bird's song is no longer heard, come take the box, little sister; in the delicate carving a pair of angels keep watch.

Don't be afraid that your thread of woven silk will be carelessly cared for.

XVII

The whole earth longs for you, Prophet of Allah, sent to wave a torch through the dark world.

I've met many wanderers, shining with the light you brought.

For me, Lord, You are the fire that has settled in my field, that has burned away the shrubs and brushwood and now is licking across to wipe out the weeds still growing there.

XVIII

What's the point to us sobbing, little sister, because our paths won't meet in that great garden?

Ah, right now aren't we picking blossoms, beautiful ornaments, my little sister, to decorate the lovely loose knot of your hair?

I'm gathering blossoms, and flowers too, and then you'll braid them to adorn the Dwelling where His belovèd comes to celebrate.

XIX

I laugh, hearing you sigh. Pardon me, little sister.

You still don't know who I am.

Stealing, grabbing, knocking things apart, used to be my trade. I've stormed palaces and castles, I've used them strictly for my own pleasure.

Once I was stranded, sucked down, then thrown up by the rolling waves.

It was only His love that kept me from being floated away, that sent me drifting toward the Island of Hope.

And now I'm simply a wanderer, taking comfort from Your light even as I shiver. I'm still not ready to go sailing to that far-off ever-bright shore.

XX

The scent of the pineapples in front of my house, the smell of the tiny white flowers along the side road, ah, why does the pure fragrance carry me swellingly off?

XXI

You up there, Cloud . . .

People are happy, staring up at you; but the penniless wanderer slips back into memory.

Hey you, Cloud . . . in the blazing heat, in the bright twilight . . . you're a sight that only wanderers really see.

XXIII

I push my bike, alone.

The sky is clear, the water glitters in the heaped-up sunlight.

I hear laughter and whispers. A rickshaw passes.

Ah, I'm swept into a world of remembering, on the bridge, the rain pouring down . . .

XXV

If so it must be, oh God of mine, I'd better bow my head.

Perhaps that's not the path I was going to take.

I submit, in order that my path cross Yours.

XXVI

I sit patiently, with crossed legs, along the side of the road.

The broiling heat, the pouring rain, the wind-blown dust, I don't notice them.

I wait, fixed, unmoving . . . , although the king of the day has dropped down, although the queen of the night is climbing to her throne.

I wait.

May You, Belovèd, come past, brushing me with Your robe, Your loving gown.

TRANSLATED BY BURTON RAFFEL AND NURDIN SALAM

J(ohannes) E. Tatengkeng

BORN on October 19, 1907, in eastern Indonesia, and a member of the country's Christian minority, Tatengkeng received an intensive education in Dutch and Dutch culture. A teacher and school administrator, both before the war and after, he taught Dutch for a time at the Zendingsstandaardschool, a missionary school on the island of Sumba, and was later principal of the Schakelschool, Ulu-Siau. In 1947 he became Minister of Education of the State of East Indonesia; in 1949 he was Minister-President. More recently he has headed the Cultural Division of the Province of Celebes (Sulawesi).

An early member of the *Pudjangga Baru* group, Tatengkeng's poetry was frequently religious, but no more parochially so than that of Amir Hamzah (as the latter was deeply loyal to Islam, so Tatengkeng is a faithful Protestant). He had begun to write *pantun* and other verse while still in elementary school; while continuing to draw on older Malay poetry, he also was much influenced by the Dutch "Generation of '80." "In fact," notes John M. Echols (*Indonesian Writing in Translation*, p. 5), "one of the distinguishing characteristics of the *Pudjangga Baru* group is the influence it received from such Dutch writers of '80 as Willem Kloos and Perk, for example." Tatengkeng's early verse features, in addition, a wry, self-critical tone (*Dipantai*, *Waktu Petang*, On the Shore: Twilight) which leads very naturally into the work of the generation following, the "Generation of '45." Tatengkeng's later poetry—witness *Penumpang Kelas I* (Traveler First Class)—shows a clear awareness of Chairil Anwar and his successors and colleagues.

Rindu Dendam (Desire), 1934.

ON THE SHORE: TWILIGHT

Dipantai, Waktu Petang

The small waves break with a splash,
The great sun flickers.
It's a quiet, pleasant day,
With blue-red mountains all around.

The fishermen's boats sail along in clusters,
Out from the bay, into the shallows:
The sailors sing melancholy songs
Of old loves, lost loves.

The sun looks down the other side of the mountains,
The moon slips grinning into its place,

And this poet goes off into musing
And praise—and gathers in a poem.

The emptier, the lonelier the world
The more yearningly the Soul sings on . . .

TRANSLATED BY BURTON RAFFEL AND NURDIN SALAM

Tatengkeng

MY FEELING FOR ART

Perasaan Seni

Like the rush of flooding water,
Like the shrill shout of the wind,
    It comes
    When it chooses,
Pouring, heaping, pushing everywhere,
Sweetening my soul, enslaving my body.

As lovely as the fresh coolness of dew,
A song as soft as the wind,
    It comes
    When it chooses,
Urging, opening me to the chanting of words,
Rowing my heart where it panted to come.

Whether you come as a giant demon
Or sweep down like beauty's own face
    I'm ready
    To serve you:
My whole body is yours,
My soul is your throne!

TRANSLATED BY BURTON RAFFEL AND NURDIN SALAM

Tatengkeng

TRAVELER FIRST CLASS

Penumpang Kelas I

Before I was thirty
I was never more than a deck passenger.
Thanks to the efforts of my friends
And the transfer of sovereignty
I'm now a traveler first class.

I'm one of the army
Of inspection officials
Wandering
From island to island
Building up the country.

Every evening I play bridge in the salon
And drink my beer
And rage at the waiter.

I've never written a report.

I disembark
And give half a rupiah
For the workers on the first of May.

TRANSLATED BY JAMES S HOLMES

Tatengkeng

Part II

ANGKATAN '45

The Generation of '45:

PIONEERS

Chairil Anwar

BORN on July 26, 1922, in Medan, Sumatra, Anwar died on April 28, 1949, in Djakarta. Family finances prevented him from going farther than the second class of the Dutch middle school (MULO), but he read widely and deeply—and in Dutch, German, English, Spanish, and French. Briefly an editor, he followed no profession but poetry.

Anwar began to write as a schoolboy, poems he later destroyed. He began to compose the poetry for which he is famous during the Japanese occupation, in 1942; the first of these fully matured, carefully worked-out poems were known only by manuscript copies passed from hand to hand. Quite simply, they effected a literary revolution. "I have heard more than one Indonesian writer say," reports John M. Echols (*Indonesian Writing in Translation*, p. 62), "that he did not realize the capabilities and potentialities of the Indonesian language until he read Chairil's poetry." Derwent May, in *Indonesian Information*, puts it this way: "Indonesian literature had never previously known such full and unguarded revelation of a personality, nor an art so apt for the task and so subtle."

Anwar wrote only seventy-odd poems (plus a few translations, speeches, and radio scripts); no collection of his work appeared during his lifetime. Although acknowledged as the driving spirit of the "Generation of '45," he was never a leader, a literary man in the style, say, of S. T. Alisjahbana. Anwar truly started nothing, founded nothing, and began (with pardonable exaggeration) everything. Together with like-minded poets and painters, he was one of the organizers of *Gelanggang* (The Arena), serving among its editors. With the poets Asrul Sani and Rivai Apin, he published (posthumously) *Tiga Menguak Takdir* (Three against Fate, or, as Derwent May renders it, Three of Us Croak Out Our Destiny; "*Takdir*" is also meant to suggest Sutan *Takdir* Alisjahbana). But for most of his brief life he was the archtype of a loner, a Bohemian, subject to no dis-

51

cipline but that of setting pen to paper. When he was admitted to a Djakarta hospital, not yet twenty-seven years old, he was suffering from syphilis, typhus, and tuberculosis simultaneously. The large number of death-poems, in one of his final notebooks, indicates how aware of his approaching end he had become. One unrevised fragment is particularly striking:

> Let's
> Leave here
> Just as we planned, just
> As we agreed
> Once
>
> And one by one
> Give up everything
> In this most progressive of worlds
>
> Before we go
> Let's strip the waving trees
> Let's shave off women's long, waving hair
>
> But don't cut down desire

Appropriately, for his verse is profoundly western-influenced, and—language apart—readily accessible to western sensibilities, Anwar was the first Indonesian poet to be featured by an American literary magazine (*Prairie Schooner*, Summer, 1962). His verse is also the first Indonesian poetry to appear in the United States in a volume of its own: *Chairil Anwar: Selected Poems* (New Directions, 1963). At its glowing best this is brilliant writing, touched at times with macabre elements, at times heated with fierce sentimentality. Anwar is, *tout court*, Indonesia's only unqualifiedly great poet, to date.

Deru Tjampur Debu (Noise Mixed with Dust), 1949; *Kerikil Tadjam dan Jang Terampas dan Jang Putus* (Sharp Gravel and Plundered and Broken), 1949; *Tiga Menguak Takdir* (Three against Fate), 1950 (with Asrul Sani and Rivai Apin); *Chairil Anwar, Pelopor Angkatan 45* (C. A., Pioneer of the Generation of '45), 1956, a critical study by H. B. Jassin, incorporating some poems not elsewhere published.

52

ME

Aku

When my time comes
I want to hear no one's cries,
Nor yours either

Away with all who cry!

Here I am, a wild beast,
Cut off from his companions

Bullets may pierce my skin
But I'll keep on,

Carrying forward my wounds and my pain,
Attacking,
Attacking,
Until suffering disappears

And I won't care anymore

I want to live a thousand years

TRANSLATED BY BURTON RAFFEL AND NURDIN SALAM

TUTI'S ICE CREAM

Tuti Artic

Between present and future happiness
The abyss gapes.
My girl is licking at her ice cream:
This afternoon you're my love,
I adorn you with cake and coca-cola
Oh wife-in-training.
We have stopped the clocks' ticking.

You kissed skillfully, indelibly.
—When we cycled I took you home
—Your blood was hot, soon you were a woman,
And the stiff old man dreamed dreams
That leaped over the moon.

Every day's beau invited you on,
Every day's beau was different.
Tomorrow we'll meet and not know each other:
Heaven is this minute's game.

I am like you, everything ran by,
Me and Tuti and Greet and Amoi . . .
Dilapidated hearts.
Love's a danger that quickly fades.

TRANSLATED BY BURTON RAFFEL AND NURDIN SALAM

AN ORDINARY SONG

Lagu Biasa

On the restaurant terrace, now, we're face to face,
Just introduced. We simply stare,
Although we've already dived into the ocean of each other's
  souls.

In this first act
We're still only looking.
The orchestra plays "Carmen" along with us.

She winks. She laughs.
And the dry grass blazes up.
She speaks. Her voice is loud,
My blood stops running.

When the orchestra begins the "Ave Maria"
I drag her over there . . .

TRANSLATED BY BURTON RAFFEL AND NURDIN SALAM

Anwar   55

IN VAIN

Sia-Sia

The last time you came
You brought bright flowers,
Red roses, white jasmine,
Blood and holiness,
And spread them in front of me
With a decisive look: for you.

We were stunned
And asked each other: what's this?
Love? Neither of us understood.

That day we were together.
We did not touch.

But my heart will not give itself to you,
And does not care
That you are ripped by desolation.

TRANSLATED BY BURTON RAFFEL AND NURDIN SALAM

WITH PATIENCE

Kesabaran

I cannot go to sleep.
Men talking, dogs *gonggong*ing.
Yet the world seems to fade,
The darkness a wall of stone
Where the voices only beat,
The fire and the ash beyond it.

There is something I want to say
But I have neither voice nor energy.
Well! it's of no importance
For the world declines to be addressed.

The river water freezes
And life is life no longer.

I think of what returned before,
Closing my eyes, closing my ears,
Waiting for the peace that must come.

TRANSLATED BY DERWENT MAY

TWILIGHT AT A LITTLE HARBOR

Sendja di Pelabuhan Ketjil

FOR SRI AJATI

This time no one's looking for love
Between the sheds, the old houses, in the make-believe
Of poles and rope. A boat, a *prau* without water,
Puffs and blows, thinking there's something it can catch.

The drizzle comes harder and darkens. There's an eagle
    flapping,
Pushing sulkily off, and the day swimming silkily
To meet temptations yet to come. Nothing moves.
And now the sand and the sea are asleep, the waves are gone.

There's no one else. I'm alone. Walking,
Combing the cape, still drowning the hope
Of just once getting to the end of it and saying goodbye to
    everything
From the fourth beach, where the last sob could be hugged
    tightly to me.

TRANSLATED BY BURTON RAFFEL AND NURDIN SALAM

NOCTURNO

Nocturno

I shouted—but no voice answered,
The sound congealed in the frozen air.
In my body desires stretched,
Dead too.
The last dream asked for power,
The axe was broken, swung in vain,
And my heart was strangled.

Stranded . . . I tasted ashes and dust
From a left-over song.
A memory of the ghostly emptiness
And the fever that will stiffen us.

.   .   .   .

Pen and poet, both dead,
Turning!

TRANSLATED BY BURTON RAFFEL AND NURDIN SALAM

LOVE IN A BROTHEL

(title supplied)

Let this evening go by, now,
My love—yet the dream still chafes away at
What has brought us together, here in this room
High as a cave and mute
As the last cold station
In that night lined with criss-crossed beds.
We lie on the one
Set furthest apart.

Our whispers don't push at time:
We kiss, I'm delighted
With everything you do,
Even though the others alongside me
Are watching from their beds
With hate in their eyes
And slack, exhausted hands.

Where's the sin, what's the mistake,
The uneasiness flooded with regret
That makes me the victim
When quickly, not hesitating, you accomplish
What I'd never consent to?
Softly you tell me
You've taken someone else
And, full of sadness, I feel myself
The odd man out, and quickly leave.

TRANSLATED BY BURTON RAFFEL AND NURDIN SALAM

Anwar

MY LOVE FAR IN THE ISLANDS

Tjintaku Djauh Dipulau

My love far in the islands,
  Loving girl,
Now passing the time alone.

The boat sails on, the moon is cool,
I carry a present round my neck,
The wind helps, the sea is clear,
Yet I know that I shall never reach her.

In the clear water, in the moaning wind,
In the feeling I have that all passes,
My death is speaking queenly words
"My lap must be your boat's harbor."

Why! how many years have I sailed
In my boat as fragile as me?
Why must my death begin to call me
Before I have kissed my love again?

My loving girl far in the islands,
  If I should die,
Will die passing the time alone.

TRANSLATED BY DERWENT MAY

MY LOVE'S ON A FAR-AWAY ISLAND

Tjintaku Djauh Dipulau

My love's on a far-away island,
A sweet girl, doing nothing for lack of anything better.

The *prau* slides quickly along, the moon gleams,
Around my neck I wear a charm for my girl;
The wind helps, the sea's clear, but I know
I'm not going to reach her.

In the calm water, in the gentle wind,
In the final sensation, everything goes swiftly.

Fate takes command, saying:
"Better steer your *prau* straight into my lap."

Hey! I've come this way for years!
The *prau* I'm in is going to crash!
Why is Fate calling
Before I have a chance to hug my girl?

My sweet on a far-away island,
If I die, she'll die for lack of anything better.

TRANSLATED BY BURTON RAFFEL AND NURDIN SALAM

Anwar

AT THE MOSQUE

Dimesdjid

I shouted at Him
Until He came.

We met face to face.

Afterwards He burned in my breast.
All my strength struggles to extinguish Him.

My body, which won't be driven, is soaked with sweat.

This room
Is the arena where we fight,

Destroying each other,
One hurling insults, the other gone mad.

TRANSLATED BY BURTON RAFFEL AND NURDIN SALAM

TO THE PAINTER AFFANDI

Kepada Pelukis Affandi

If I have run out of words, no longer
Dare to enter my own house, standing
On the crumbling doorstep,

The reason is all the world that never
Lasts, that piece by piece
Death will come to destroy.

And hands will stiffen, no longer write,
Troubled by pain, troubled by dreams.
Give me a place on a lofty tower,
Where you alone rise over

Crowds and noise and quarrels,
Over smooth selfishness and make-believe creation:
You turn away and pray
And the closed-up darkness opens!

TRANSLATED BY BURTON RAFFEL AND NURDIN SALAM

TO A FRIEND

Kepada Kawan

Before emptiness draws closer
And the final treachery leaps at us from behind,
While blood runs and feeling beats,

And despair has not bloomed and there is no fear
Remember the evening fades, without warning,
A red sail dipping into darkness,
And, friend, let's part now, here:
The emptiness that pulls at us also strangles itself!

So
Empty the glass,
Pierce, traverse, invert the world,
Love women, but leave the flatterers,
Rope the wildest horse, spur him swiftly,
Tie him to neither noon nor night
And
Undo what you've done,
End without inheritance, without family,
Without requesting forgiveness,
Without granting it!

So
Again
Let us part:
The final agony will draw us into an empty sky.
Once more, friend, one line more:
Shove your sword to the hilt
 Into those who've diluted the pureness of honey!!!

TRANSLATED BY BURTON RAFFEL AND NURDIN SALAM

Anwar   *65*

THE CAPTURED AND THE FREED

Jang Terampas dan Jang Luput

Darkness and a passing wind rake me.
I shiver, and so does the great room where the one I want is
  lying.
The night sinks in, the trees are as dead as columns of stone.

At Karet, at Karet (where I go next), the cold wind blows
  just as noisily.

I'm tidying my room, and my heart, in case you come
And I can set free a new story for you;
But now it's only my hands that move fiercely.

My body is quiet and alone, the tale and the time go stiffly,
  icily by.

TRANSLATED BY BURTON RAFFEL AND NURDIN SALAM

ANNIHILATION

Hampa

Silent outside. A silence that presses and pushes.
The trees straight and stiff, still to their crests.
A silence that snaps. Not a breath of power to pull
The world into new shapes. Everything waiting.

A silence growing as it waits until it is able
To bury its weight into all things until all vanish.
Poisoned air. Satan shrieking. The silence
Continues, and continues to wait.

TRANSLATED BY DERWENT MAY

Anwar

HEAVEN

Sorga

Like my mother, and my grandmother too,
Plus seven generations before them,
I also seek admission to heaven,
Which the Moslem Party and the Mohammedan Party say
   has rivers of milk
And thousands of houris all over.

But there's a contemplative voice inside me,
Stubbornly mocking: Can you ever
Get dry after a soaking in the blue sea,
After the sly temptations waiting in every port?
Anyway, who can say for sure
That there really are houris there
With voices as rich and husky as Nina's, with eyes that flirt
   like Jati's?

TRANSLATED BY BURTON RAFFEL AND NURDIN SALAM

A TALE FOR DIEN TAMAELA

Tjerita Buat Dien Tamaela

I am Pattiradjawane
Whom the gods watch over,
I alone.

I am Pattiradjawane,
Foam of the sea.
The sea is my blood.

I am Pattiradjawane:
When I was born
The gods brought me an oar.

I am Pattiradjawane, guarding the nutmeg groves.
I am fire on the shore. Whoever comes near
Must call my name three times.

In the night-time quiet, seaweed dances
To the sound of my drum,
Nutmeg trees become maidens' bodies
And live till dawn.

Dance!
Be happy!
Forget everything!

But take care not to make me angry.
I'll kill the nut trees, stiffen the maidens,
I'll bring down the gods!

Anwar   69

I'm in the night, in the day,
In the rhythm of the seaweed and in the fire that roasts the
   island . . .

I am Pattiradjawane
Whom the gods watch over,
I alone.

TRANSLATED BY BURTON RAFFEL AND NURDIN SALAM

Anwar

Rivai Apin

BORN on August 30, 1927, in Padang Pandjang, Sumatra, Apin graduated from upper middle school (SMA) and for a time studied law in Djakarta. He has worked as a police assistant (and as a black marketeer), but for the most part his occupation has been that of an editor. He served in the latter capacity with *Nusantara, Zenith, Gelanggang* (The Arena—see under Chairil Anwar, above), *Siasat,* and *Gema Suasana;* now a member of the secretariat of LEKRA, or Lembaga Kebudajaan Rakjat (People's Cultural League), he is editor of that organization's cultural magazine, *Zaman Baru* (New Era).

Closely associated with Chairil Anwar, Apin has published comparatively little poetry. Unlike Anwar, however, he has exerted a very considerable influence on the Indonesian literary scene by extraliterary means, principally by his work as an editor. Always deeply concerned with social issues, Apin has sharply affected his poetic output by adopting the literary stance of the Communist Party, "social realism." Says Bakri Siregar (*Penjair dan Sandjak,* p. 86), "Rivai Apin has now become an adherent of the ideology of social realism, which he feels more appropriate to a revolutionary outlook." At its best, Apin's work expresses a powerfully charged social sense in strong, complex language; the poems which follow are some of the most intellectual verse ever written by an Indonesian.

Tiga Menguak Takdir (Three against Fate), 1950 (with Chairil Anwar and Asrul Sani).

BETWEEN TWO UNFINISHED WORLDS

Dari Dua Dunia Belum Sudah

That morning I heard the news,
I went into the street.
Peddlers and people trying to go to work hugged the edges
    of the road;
Speeding cars, heavy with soldiers, and tanks, met no resist-
    ance.

Soldiers patrolled, marching two by two, carrying guns,
And among them an eighty-eight, but a loaded one!
Everything jumbled together:
Men, and things, and the air, each hung with its price-tag.

I went to friends, to talk; the truth turned into blackness.
The news: Djokja [1] had fallen, Maguwo . . . Karno [2] was
    captured,
Hatta, Sjahrir [3] . . .
We talked on, or went from friend to friend to friend . . .
We talked, we thought, and we discovered hope,
All of it in one Word [4] and because of one Word.

That evening I went home, burdened with the news and
    our hope.
I was greeted by my unfinished self:
Open books, unread books, books I had
To finish—
But for this I had left my father and my brother—

[1] At that time the capital of the Indonesian Republic; the struggle was against Indonesia's former colonial masters, the Dutch.
[2] President Soekarno.
[3] Respectively, the former vice-president and the leader of the
banned Socialist Party; both men are former prime ministers.
[4] Freedom (*merdeka*).

Apin

And then I remembered I had eaten only once that day.
—The pot of rice was there all along— And the self
I had been
Lay in its hollow grave, dug by the glow of a lamp
Burning in the darkness.

That night there was the sound of boots kicking against the
    wall
In the darkness.
And when the soldiers had gone there was the sound of
    weeping women,
Wives and mothers.
I don't need to tell who was taken away.
All I could do was pound my head against the table,
Tortured by that Word, rootless but already growing in its
    unfinished world.

TRANSLATED BY JEAN KENNEDY AND BURTON RAFFEL

Apin 73

POEMS FOR A LITTLE SISTER: IV

Sadjak Buat Adik: Sadjak IV

The days are getting shorter,
Fingers stiffen, chilled by the night
They cannot give things their final shape.

Can we still hear
The old dreams singing?
Must we?
Let the twilight cover over the day
And we'll watch with our stiff eyes.

Tomorrow there'll be another day
But it will be getting shorter.

TRANSLATED BY BURTON RAFFEL AND NURDIN SALAM

POEMS FOR A LITTLE SISTER: VI

Sadjak Buat Adik: Sadjak VI

The women and children have already sensed
That moment when everything stops.

Yet everyone's busily fixing
The red earth with its crosses.

We've come, sadly, with our thin bags
Of leather and bones,
All of us bent under a cross.

In the darkness of the valley of defeat
We struggle with the cross
And it isn't hard to forget
Just what we're suffering for.

TRANSLATED BY BURTON RAFFEL AND NURDIN SALAM

INDEPENDENCE

Kebebasan

Upon the ruins of the wall I myself tumbled down
I rein in my white horse, graceful and proud.
In front of me stretch fields and hills
With the curve of the sky that makes me hunger for open
    spaces.

Then the heart that clangs
In my chest finds room there
And spins out the blood it's been pounding and beating.

My horse's blood goes wild, too, and he rears with frustra-
    tion.
I give him his head and, bellowing, we rush toward the
    beaches.

TRANSLATED BY BURTON RAFFEL AND NURDIN SALAM

SON OF THE NIGHT

Anak Malam

FOR LIES

I

The evening wind shivers,
Blown to shreds at the end of the meaningless road;
The fence around the bridge is cold in my hands
In the moment of my waking: onto what wet shore have I
    been cast?

There's nothing to lean down on, in the dark ravine.
I hear the barking yelp of my cough.
My desire is bloodless;
It no longer hopes, now.

And on the restaurant terrace
I sing
Of all the sorrow you buried away, that time.

This dismal land's not mine,
The place I dream of is always green.

Why did I start on this journey,
Life that knows neither brightness nor light?

II

When the guard changed
The wind was lying in emptiness;
I'm the only one standing,
Valueless, worthless.

I turn up my jacket lapel:
There's no wind, it's not cold.
The air is dull and tasteless.
I move, but only because I feel like it,
Once I dreamed very different things.

Far away, in the Ocean of the North, they hear
A sail flapping, beaten by the wind;
I lift myself higher, higher, and see
There *is* something flashing by.

I look at my hands. At my bony
Skin and blue veins
And at myself:
What made me turn into this?

III
Puddles of water and patches of grass along the road;
Walking in the darkness all you can feel
Is blackness pulled down over everything by the evening
    wind,
Bright yellow swinging from the lamp posts.

I let the light that swings toward me go free.
Suddenly there's a clear pure calm beside me,
My lips stop trembling the way they did when I spoke
    before
Because they have no faith in the footprints I've left behind.

Now I have no direction.
It makes no difference where I am
And I can go where I like.
No one's strong enough to tie me down
Or set me free
And not only not strong enough, but helpless, too.

TRANSLATED BY BURTON RAFFEL AND NURDIN SALAM

Apin

POEMS FOR A LITTLE SISTER: XIII

Sadjak Buat Adik: Sadjak XIII

Don't look for us here among the corpses.
We're with those who are alive;
We'll never die,
We'll never die.

We, you, you and you . . . .
       All of us!
We've never turned and looked at death
Because the soul does not die.

We've never wanted to turn,
Hoping for the gift of mercy.
We don't know what it is to feel longing;
Our wings will never carry us back home.

We don't want to weep and mourn.
All around us there's a time of brightness, certain forever.
Because we don't want to think
We only know
Our strength is rushing to throw itself down.

This time is time only for this time,
But it will pass;
This place is a place only for this place,
But it will be left behind.

We don't expect to want to turn back;
We're delighted
To shape ourselves according to the time and the place
And to rush forward to throw ourselves down,
And to rush forward to throw ourselves down.

TRANSLATED BY BURTON RAFFEL AND NURDIN SALAM

A MONUMENT

Tugu

When the house and the dream have been destroyed
Don't say:
The cattle are dead, all that was lovely has faded,
And you're alone, staring out at the proof of it. Remember!
This time will have its monument, carved with words for a
  beginning and words for an end.

Let no one go home with blood and tears:
Sprinkle them over the earth, they'll raise up a gleaming
  thing.
Stones of defeat on top of stones of defeat
Will become a towering column
On which we shall carve victory.

TRANSLATED BY BURTON RAFFEL AND NURDIN SALAM

Apin

THE BROKEN BRIDGE

Djembatan Patah

Night falls in the middle of the day

I

Close, close, my eyes;
Close, heart.
Gripped in night's hard hands I'm afraid—
When the branches brush against my roof,
When I hear the heavy breath of the wind,
Crickets' screams, dogs' yelping,
God doesn't exist and men have nothing to say.

There are those who are happy in their houses,
With warm pillows, mattress and blanket.
There are those who lie scattered on the floor of the market-
   place.
There are probably some, too,
Who are working—maybe in a printing shop.

I don't know!
Close, close, my eyes.
I wish all of this were worth something,
That pillow, that mattress and blanket,
The cold floor and the work.
Ah close, my heart,
Close, my heart:
God doesn't exist and men have nothing to say . . .

II

There were some who weren't shot dead:
Some soldiers die without being wounded.

Apin   81

Love congeals to fill every corner,
Today's fire's finished, there is no flame,
Words are dead souls,
Space contained and stiff;
The lungs heave, panting and panting.

Some there are not stricken down dead:
Some soldiers die without being wounded.

Oh to be able
To fill the silent space when the excitement's over—
Not this victory time after time,
But only some door that's always open.

TRANSLATED BY JAMES S HOLMES, BURTON RAFFEL,
AND NURDIN SALAM

ELEGY (to an older poet)

Elegi

What we can feel, but need not mention,
What we can think, but need not say . . .
Don't grieve—we shall go on,
We shall bring this truth to its star and its earth.
And we are sure, having preserved one of your words,
One sight of a barren land, before sorrow choked our hearts.
Oh, your memory will always pursue us,
Frightening as a shadow in the swaying hut, when the lamp
    is lit,
But as full of love as the Father's outstretched hands;
And you come back, as in the days when you and this world
    still rang with life.
We shall not forget you, hunting or running,
Since what we pursue and what we run from
Is what you'll die for
And how we'll reflect on you.
And we know, too, as you know, that there is no idol and no
    other God worth living for.
Let the storm blow in this barren desert:
Our buried feet in this arid land, where you are lying,
Continue to flare, and we that stand here are flames.
We maintain Life for tonight, the night which will become
    noon.
We are sons of one Father,
We are sons of one Mother,
And though our death is only a matter of time
We shall all uphold the One God.
Brothers yet to come, brothers already gone,
We shall lift this cracked earth, this dry earth,
A heavy burden for aching shoulders—and our hearts, bitter
    with defeat,
Will fill with love for the belief we follow.

TRANSLATED BY BURTON RAFFEL AND NURDIN SALAM

Asrul Sani

BORN on June 10, 1926, in Rao, Sumatra, Sani was trained as a veterinary doctor but has never practiced his profession. During the revolutionary period he first led nonprofessional troops, then joined the Indonesian Army. Essayist, critic, and writer of short stories, as well as poet, Sani has helped edit *Gema Suasana, Zenith, Siasat,* and *Gelanggang* (The Arena—see under Chairil Anwar, above). In 1947 he founded and edited the daily resistance newspaper, *Suara Bogor* (The Voice of Bogor).

Much interested in drama, he was one of the founders and has been the Director of Indonesia's National Theatrical Academy. In addition to producing and directing motion pictures, he has done a good deal of translating: Sartre's *Huis Clos,* García Lorca's *The Blood Wedding,* Sherwood's *Petrified Forest,* and Vercors' *Le Silence de la Mer.* He studied in Europe in 1952 and again in 1953, and spent a year in the United States under a grant from the Rockefeller Foundation.

Sani's approach to poetry has come to be directly opposed to that now espoused by Rivai Apin (see above). In his own words: "For me, egoism in literature is a free gift to man-kind—which has been almost entirely devoured by ma-chines, by routines, and by politicians who know only gen-eralities and know nothing of variety." For Sani, accord-ingly, a poem is a poem, not a political manifesto.

Tiga Menguak Takdir (Three against Fate), 1950 (with Chairil Anwar and Rivai Apin).

REMEMBER FATHER, REMEMBER FATHER

Kenanglah Bapa, Kenanglah Bapa

"Let us take the north road!"
    "Brother, that is not the north."
"Ah, then my child has been taken to the south."

Gone on horseback to the South,
Racing, racing, racing through the black night.
Even while we were all as close as brothers
My child was carried away
And I was killed.

"Let us take the south road!"
    "No, brother, that is not the south."
"Ah, then, my loved one has been taken southeast."

You know the love of every father
And what he hopes for his children.
Now all hope and love are gone.
The wind from the sea has blown with a far-off sadness.

"Bring all the troops to the southeast!"
    "My friend, that is not the way."
"Ah, where, where have you taken my child?"

You!—you who were my loved one!
Who is there to guide you,
To show you that shadows are not substance,
That the sun is not God,
And that to hope is to acquiesce.

Listen, listen, here is the suffering of man!
He asks for good fortune
And yet curses, curses at whoever has sinned . . . .

86   *Sani*

Yes, friend, I have damned my own brother,
Because love
Knows no brother.

I take all my curses back:
Let my brother pass in peace.
And to you who heard what I said
I confess: "I was not killed by my brother,
I killed myself."

"Brother, where is the right, where is the left, where is the
        middle road?"
    "Yes, the three run in all directions."
"I want to follow them, everywhere."

Peace, peace be with you, brother,
Galloping, galloping down the shining street.
And you, little one, on your mother's knee,
If grow you will,
Play carefully with your glass beads;
As soon as you know how to laugh
Then remember father—remember father . . . . !

TRANSLATED BY JEAN KENNEDY

Sani   87

A MOTHER'S LETTER

Surat Dari Ibu

Go into the far-flung world, my belovèd son!
Go to a free life!
While the wind is at your back,
And the morning is bright on the leaves,
And in the jungles and on the green fields.

Go over the open sea, my belovèd son,
Go to a free world!
Before the day darkens
And the reddening dusk
Shuts the door of the Past.

When shadows fade away,
And gulls return to their nests,
And the wind blows toward land,
And the masts dry themselves,
And the skipper has lost his compass,
Then you can return!

Return, my belovèd son,
To the evening's side,
And when your ship draws up to the quay
We shall speak
"About love and your life in the morning."

TRANSLATED BY BURTON RAFFEL AND NURDIN SALAM

Sani

Siti Nuraini

SITI NURAINI is one of three women poets represented in this volume. Although she has published very little lately, she continues to write, and has been working for some time on a novel. Her early poetry, written while she was still in her teens, was published in *Siasat* (Inquiry), a magazine which she and Asrul Sani helped edit; her work appeared in the postwar issues of *Pudjangga Baru* and in *Mimbar Indonesia*.

A WOMAN

Perempuan

A woman who languidly breaks
a dry twig, leaning out of the high
rectangular window; a distant secret
calls, an odd sensation touches her heart.

Her soul is occupied, a lake lies open,
a second world at the border of her being.
Love and longing roll
in the deeps, never once coming to the surface.

Her bleak house, embraced by solitude,
chases away the birds into the night.
She herself shivers, hesitates
at the threshold, panics, then in time
jerks the door open, and her face falls closed.

TRANSLATED BY JAMES S HOLMES

Nuraini

Mohammad Akbar Djuhana

BORN IN 1925, in Tandjung Balai, Sumatra, Djuhana (or Djoehana) has long been active in government service. After graduating from secondary school, and before the Dutch military action of July, 1947, he headed the division of Youth Affairs in the Ministry of Information, Djakarta. He has served as secretary to Sutan Sjahrir, formerly Prime Minister and himself a man of sensitivity and good taste in literary matters. Djuhana has held a variety of diplomatic posts, including service with UNESCO in Paris.

In 1948 Djuhana was the editor of *Opbouw*, but went abroad the next year, studying Eastern languages at the Sorbonne, Paris. Writing in both Indonesian and Dutch, he prefers the latter.

POÈTE MAUDIT

Poète Maudit

Writing! One should not be writing on a night like this!
The dark sky; the windows rattling in the wind;
Something crying as if for some shelter that it cannot find;
What, I cannot tell.

Mechanically my thoughts drift away
And unconsciously the stream flows back to childhood.
I understand this dreaming—but why
Must I keep on writing in the dark?

How inevitably this question forms
Itself (though dinner is scarcely finished),
Only to disappear again, without an answer.
And my conscience, how meticulous! how hedged-in!

One cannot just sit dreaming
When the bullets whistle one by one,
And somehow must begin to write.

TRANSLATED BY AHMED ALI AND IDHAM

Djuhana

Joke Moeljono

BORN on July 30, 1925, in Bandung, Java, Moeljono studied
medicine for several years at the Medical Faculty, Djakarta;
in August, 1946, he went to Amsterdam to continue his
medical training. After some years abroad, he returned to
Bandung, where he works at the Pasteur Institute as a
pathologist.

Although much of his poetry is in Dutch (including the
poem which follows), Moeljono is fully alive to *bahasa Indonesia* and to the work being written in it. During his stay
in Amsterdam, indeed, he was responsible for introducing
the Indonesian language and its vital new literature to the
American critic, editor, and translator, James S Holmes.

The translation of *Zij* (She) which follows is based on a
slightly different version from that originally printed in a
Dutch periodical in 1950. Moeljono intends this as yet un-
published new version to supersede the original.

SHE

She was the plaintiff, but she took
A lover after the divorce.
He was dark and slenderer,
Defter at loving.

His successors were of various hues,
Europe sated herself on Asia,
Fourth floor in Amsterdam South:
But—Africa called.

Last time I saw her on the Dam,
Blonde as the moon,
With a black giant
Of a Negro.

TRANSLATED BY JAMES S HOLMES

Moeljono

Louise Walujati Hatmoharsoio

BORN on December 5, 1924, in Sukabumi, Java, Walujati was educated in her native city and in Bogor. Her mother was a devout Moslem; her father leaned toward theosophy. At the age of thirteen she began to write poetry in Dutch; when the Japanese invaded Indonesia she studied Japanese poetry, at the same time working as an elementary school teacher.

"After the proclamation of independence," on August 17, 1945, writes H. B. Jassin (*Gema Tanah Air*, Echoes of Our Land, p. 236), "she began to work in the social field. From childhood on she has been deeply concerned with the world about her. Fond of painting, and an amateur musician . . . she is drawn to books of philosophy and theosophy." After the war, and with minimal preparation, Walujati began to write poetry in Indonesian. In 1951 she published a novel, *Pudjani*; most of her poetry, notes Bakri Siregar (*Penjair dan Sandjak*, p. 83), predates her marriage.

PARTING

Berpisah

Together we braid flowers
Into a delicate, fragrant bouquet,
Returning home, happy,
As the red ball drops down from the sky.

At the side-road we part.
The bouquet trembles in our hands,
Falls, and breaks into two.

I take one half, you the other
And, holding it firmly, you are gone . . .

I walk alone in the dusk,
You run away with only the flower
Sending its scent to me.

TRANSLATED BY BURTON RAFFEL AND NURDIN SALAM

Hatmoharsoio

Part III

ANGKATAN '45

The Generation of '45:

THE LATER IMPULSE

Sitor Situmorang

BORN on October 2, 1924, in Harianboho, Sumatra, Sitor was educated in Djakarta. After the Japanese invasion he worked in Medan, and later in Jogjakarta and Djakarta, as a freelance journalist and literary critic, affiliating with a variety of newspapers and periodicals. In 1952 he served briefly with the Indonesian Embassy in Paris; he had spent most of the two previous years in Holland. Returning to Indonesia, he worked for almost a year with Sticusa, a Dutch intercultural organization, in Djakarta. He has since worked with the Djawatan Kebudajaan (Cultural Division) of the Ministry of Education, Djakarta, and was for a time an appointed member of the Indonesian Parliament, representing the intellectual group rather than a political party.

Much interested in drama, and an essayist and writer of short stories as well as a poet, Sitor has published widely in all four forms. A volume of short stories, *Pertempuran dan Saldju di Paris* (Snow and Fighting in Paris), appeared in 1956; a play, *Djalan Mutiara* (Street of Pearls), in 1954. A film scenario on the revolution, *Darah dan Doa* (Blood and Prayer), was published in 1950. Sitor's interest in drama took him to the United States, under a grant from the Rockefeller Foundation; he studied at Yale University. (In the words of Asrul Sani, "The Literary Movement," *Perspective of Indonesia*, 1956, p. 47: "One significant new trend is a growing interest in the possibilities of poetic drama. Old Malay poetry was composed for recitation and is rich in symbolic content. From this tradition might well come an awakening in the drama.")

As a poet, Sitor is Chairil Anwar's direct and principal heir: his work extends and deepens the legacy Chairil left him. "Chairil Anwar died in 1949," noted Derwent May (*Eastern World*, November, 1960), ". . . but he has already had innumerable successors. Of these the most important is probably a fellow Sumatran, Sitor Situmorang."

Sitor's poetry is warmer and specifically more compassionate than Anwar's; his range is accordingly greater, doubly so because he is a more conscious and intellectual writer as well. Whether he will solidify and deepen his poetic achievement cannot be predicted, for while Anwar was wholly a poet, Sitor is drawn in many directions, politics among them.

Sitor Situmorang is a Protestant.

Surat Kertas Hidjau (Letters on Yellow Paper), 1953; *Dalam Sadjak* (In Verse), 1955; *Wadjah Tak Bernama* (Face without a Name), 1955; *Zaman Baru* (New Era), 1962.

ROOM NO. 2

Kamar II: 5 Rue Jouvenet, 4ᵐᵉ

Face that looks at me now,
Now that the doors are shut,
You are present only in absence.
All is still, over there,
And I the forgotten bridegroom.

What is it that parts
The present from the past?
No poem could guess
What is buried in its words,
Like "you who are present in absence."

Words are only windows,
Always closed,
In a thousand cities.

TRANSLATED BY DERWENT MAY

DAWN

Fadjar

There is a sorrow that rises like a tide.
The heart within never sinks
Before the edge of the last beach disappears:
The heart reaches out to the end.

On the line furthest out,
As far as the light goes,
The wind plucks a lovely tune.
Dawn never comes.

TRANSLATED BY JEAN KENNEDY AND BURTON RAFFEL

THOUSAND MOUNTAIN, JOGJA

Gunung Seribu Jogja

A dry wind fills the sky,
Leaving love's harvest
On the golden slopes of a lovely dawn,
Spreading into heaven's shining space.

The wanderer's face catches
Morning sunshine bursting
Like songs through the dry fall leaves. Frozen
Pebbles glitter in the dry river,

A current begins. In among the dry foliage.
Forgiveness is a long road:
It doesn't flow along the river bed,
And finally it turns back to sand.

TRANSLATED BY JEAN KENNEDY AND BURTON RAFFEL

SACRÉ CŒUR

Sacré Cœur

Free from an all-night party
After careless gaiety inside
Dawn brings us to morning's hill,
While the city still sleeps, to climb up above the earth.

With blood surging in dancing rhythm
Across a narrow bridge of words hardened into silence
Your eyes see the sights of morning spread out,
But as for me, I stare unsatisfied.

From the eastern sky, as usual,
The light of a new day scatters;
One by one birds sing, blue
In a heaven that does not exist.

I remember words that lead to love
At the first confession: Because of you
I've sensed life and known sorrow;
I'll never leave you again.

On my face is surprise: How can it be,
How can man surrender himself this way?
My heart, like yours, doesn't believe it,
Though we both know it without speaking.

At the song of a bird the world turns,
When you speak the day whirls to a stop
And surrenders the choice between itself
And death, which plants its seeds in the sprouting young
  morning.

While you mourn
The trees begin to bloom.

TRANSLATED BY JEAN KENNEDY AND BURTON RAFFEL

CLEAR RIVER

Sungai Bening

Your body that is firm and familiar,
Soft to my touch,
Dampens the mirror with memories come clear:
Though drenched inside, I am still dry.

After so long, I know
That nothing has moved on;
Everything is more painful and swollen,
Like a knife wound clotted together.

I am torn and cracked.
In the spout of desire
My blood thickens.

TRANSLATED BY JEAN KENNEDY AND BURTON RAFFEL

FLOWERS OF STONE

Bunga Batu

You know my feelings better than my ways.
Silence says more than sorrow.
Because whoever is left is so faithful
Knowledge finally turns to stone.

Here above flowers grow
Beautiful, as beautiful as your face;
Fragrant memories as bitter as gall,
Dark blood that dyes the soul.

A thousand years before us and after
Men will dig from within the ground
A face printed on layers of stone,
Lined with the story of death—and still unhappy.

TRANSLATED BY JEAN KENNEDY

QUATRAIN (untitled)

In two versions

Version 1

Deep in the bottom of the soul is a shallow sky
Filled with song and sweet words,
A continent always wrapped in mist,
Vague, grieving, growing more and more shallow.

TRANSLATED BY JEAN KENNEDY

Version 2

Deep in the heart there is a small country
Full of songs with sweet words to them,
A world hidden always by drizzling rain,
Obscure, coaxing, each day growing smaller.

TRANSLATED BY DERWENT MAY

Situmorang

NOTES ON 1953

Tjatatan Tahun 53

In the cave the only cry
Is the endless echo
Of paralyzed stone
(Water dripping down, drop by drop):
Let us be still, drowning,
Telling stories, in the dark,
Of life and of the forgotten one
(The light outside is lonelier than we are).

TRANSLATED BY BURTON RAFFEL

Situmorang

LA RONDE: I

La Ronde: I

Humming, to forget last night's encounter
With myself, parting in the room.
Late in the season, time for snow
To fall, hunger to grow.

Two memories, disembodied,
Come so alive I can smell them:
"Death must be like this," one whispers softly
At the height of delight, just at daybreak,

Lying on the evening's breast. "You're all mine,"
Moaning seconds flow into kisses,
Angry lips grope for time
To squeeze it into the body of a woman.

Late in the season, just at daybreak,
The open window shows fallen snow.

TRANSLATED BY JEAN KENNEDY

LA RONDE: II

La Ronde: II

Is there anything more beautiful
Than their firm, dry lips?
Is there anything sweeter
Than the darkness in the shadow of their brows?

Brows that make a painter hesitate:
To kiss or conceal that shoulder?
But the hair leads the hand
As far as the buttocks, full of suggestion.

Then the thigh, chiselled marble
Supporting the curving stomach.
Turning at the navel, then sloping
A little below, to the center of all,

Black as night, ready to accept
A beautiful supposition.
Ah, breast softly pressing my heart,
Receive
This man's overripe dream!

TRANSLATED BY JEAN KENNEDY

SWIMMING POOL

Kolam Berenang

FOR RULAN

The child and I are stretched out
Carelessly on the edge of the pool,
Examining clouds in the blue sky
As if to find some special sign.

Reflected in the clear pool
I see the calm clarity of a face
Long since silenced and gone
But not yet pronounced dead.

Then the child asks of his own accord
If men go to heaven
When they die.

And because I know for sure
I nod quietly
And the child immediately understands.

TRANSLATED BY JEAN KENNEDY AND BURTON RAFFEL

MORNING

Pagi

Long before morning the sky splits,
The party is over. Only a pool
Of spilled wine is left, like blood.
The morning is red and festering.

To catch the sunlight in the hollow of my breast
I watch the day rise on the horizon,
Piercing my heart with its sharp bullet:
Consciousness will die, my bones roar.

Adieu! Night is Hell's party!
Bonjour! The new day is shining!

Adieu! The world is a haughty lover!
I expect death for my New Love!

TRANSLATED BY JEAN KENNEDY AND BURTON RAFFEL

PARIS—AVRIL

Paris Avril: Jardin des Tuileries

FOR SUKARTINI

The lovers have come back
Along with the first bird
Coming from a far country,
Whistled by the clear air.

Amongst the ubiquitous green
The buds break into flower
And in the anxious heart
Grows a longing for youth.

We circle among the trees
Charged with the swaying questions,
Repeating once again
All that is not for ever.

TRANSLATED BY DERWENT MAY

PASTORAL

Pastoral

In the woods that morning
Long will the story be told
Of the girl who freed song
And color to the birds,

Of the season that spread out
Naked as the morning of birth
To catch all the sunshine
On the rustling leaves.

She poured out her heart,
All on a day,
She climbed a sloping hill
To splash her unripe blood all across the ravine,
In the valley one day.

TRANSLATED BY JEAN KENNEDY

Situmorang

A WOMAN'S SONG

Lagu Perempuan

When you sing like this
There is nothing else to hope for.
I believe that victory
Is for you who mourn.

Oh, faithful woman
Surely this song, trembling through your whole body,
In an intensity of grief,
Opens your way to dawn:
Later, when it is all over
And love is at your feet,
Clumsy and bleeding,
You accept it kneeling, your head bowed.

TRANSLATED BY JEAN KENNEDY AND BURTON RAFFEL

MORNING MEADOW: SUKABUMI

Lapangan Pagi, Sukabumi

There are rows of fir trees in front of the inn,
And flowers, and a deserted field.
In back the road goes down to the river.
Farther back is a highway to the city.

Morning clouds on the slope of the mountain over there:
Children come to play ball in the field;
The sun grows brighter;
Noisy cheering echoes.

As far as the eye sees there are only mountains,
As far as the mind soars there is only greenness.
I suppose I was asleep, I suppose I was dreaming a while
    ago,
Awakened but not yet awake—

The bell in the barracks next door seemed to ring loud and
    clear:
One P.M., half a day gone.
The room is very light, now,
But there could have been nothing in that empty field.

I shiver. In a corner where my mind can't reach
Night lingers with a chill.

TRANSLATED BY JEAN KENNEDY AND BURTON RAFFEL

VISIT TO A GRAVE IN A MOUNTAIN CHURCH

Ziarah Dalam Geredja Gunung

Wherever I go, I feel that you are
The only shadow.
Are you really all alone here
In the hollow chill of this isolated church?

The trilling of a bird worshipping morning
Filters into this dank hall.
What if I were here, just me
And the cold air the sun never warms.

Amen.

TRANSLATED BY JEAN KENNEDY AND BURTON RAFFEL

PINE TREES AND TOADSTOOLS

Tjemara dan Tjendawan

In the morning I see you as clearly
As the mountains against the bright sky,
Sketched sharply, shining,
Overwhelming everything in sight.

Then you slip away from me.
But I can follow your trail through the pines,
Through the clinging, rustling grass,
Sniffing after your flowered perfume.

I know you're a child, fond of being pursued,
Who likes to hide behind bushes.
I pass by, pretending not to notice,
Then come back—and find
Only a gray toadstool.

TRANSLATED BY JEAN KENNEDY AND BURTON RAFFEL

WAKING

Bangun

His sleep: for prostitutes.
His waking: for loneliness to be fed.
The poison spreads through his body,
He doesn't complain.

He creeps to the window,
Watching the morning just as he always does.
He sees trees blossoming with fruit,
A world growing more and more beautiful.

He grows gloomier.
Longing sweeps over him.

Turning to a woman's breast
He dreams of a different paradise.

TRANSLATED BY JEAN KENNEDY AND BURTON RAFFEL

CLOCK

Djam

Peaceful, alone in the quiet room,
He glances at his newspaper.
It falls. He forgets whatever's outside,
And the sun, too, that goes on shining.

The quiet slips into his thoughts.
Everything seems overcome by sleep:
Furniture, walls, and scattered memories
Fuse in vague forgetfulness.

Then in his dream the sound of the clock,
A remembered ticking.
Nothing rustling,

Only the ticking echoing inside him,
Bouncing out of the depths of his consciousness,
Emptier and emptier.

TRANSLATED BY JEAN KENNEDY AND BURTON RAFFEL

THE CHILD AND TIME

Anak dan Waktu

The Child stops to look at the clock,
To really think in silence,
Disturbed for a moment by the significance
Of its striking day and night.

But the Child doesn't want to ask:
Busily returning to his games
He forgets having wanted
To know why time exists.

The Father stretches wearily,
His voice glued to time,

His memories pursued,
But by what he does not know.

TRANSLATED BY JEAN KENNEDY AND BURTON RAFFEL

M.S. BALI

M.S. "Bali"

Day after day the beach is marshy. The boats unload.
Then load. True, there's nothing beautiful in boredom.
Stinking dregs foul every harbor.

Day after day in the middle of the sea. Evening after eve-
    ning, restless.
With the mosquitoes that poison the hot sky.
The Sea of the Dead. Strewn with corpses wound in no
    decent shrouds.

The twilight fades. There's nothing golden
In glances pallid with malaria's poison,
Assaying the brightness in other people's eyes.

There is an answer. That which waits in every harbor.
Every evening. When work is through,
After you ask, if fate has made up its mind
The fading evening will turn golden.
The end is in the clear morning, is in the sea.

Before it comes, shall we go, clearing away the trees, the
    mud,
Singing of our longing for the land of our Ancestors . . . . .
A *singsing so, a singsing so, a singsing so* . . . . .

TRANSLATED BY JEAN KENNEDY AND BURTON RAFFEL

Toto Sudarto Bachtiar

BORN on October 12, 1929, in Paliaman, Tjirebon, Java, Bachtiar graduated from upper middle school (SMA), Bandung, Java. During the revolution he joined the Tentara Nasional Indonesia (Indonesian Army). After 1950 he began the study of law at the University of Indonesia, Djakarta, and also became editor of *Madjalah Angkasa* (Air Force Magazine), official organ of the Indonesian Air Force. Bachtiar has served on the editorial staffs of *Gelanggang* (The Arena—see under Chairil Anwar, Part II), *Zenith*, and *Mimbar Indonesia.*

Clearly a member of the Generation of '45, Bachtiar is probably as much influenced by Sitor Situmorang's work as by that of Chairil Anwar. In his two volumes of verse he blends a wry, Anwar-like strength with the warmth and insight of Sitor, adding a haunting lyric grace very much his own.

Suara (A Voice), 1956; *Etsa*, 1958.

TO A DEAD MAN

Kepada Orang Mati

If you can forgive me, since forgiving is good,
You can never understand yourself.
If I forgive you, since forgiving is good,
You do not understand yourself.

So much forgiveness, for so many sins,
So many sins, for so much forgiveness,
Are they only for use among the dead,
In that airless, loveless place?

But if after all I should not forgive you
That would be reason for true sorrow—
Not understanding myself,
Not understanding you,
Only wanting not to die now, so young.

TRANSLATED BY DERWENT MAY

Bachtiar

NIGHT AT SEA

Malam Laut

Because the sea never gives up, I am the sea.
Because the sea tells no lies, I am the sea.
It's very close but very lonely:
Catch it, then it's free again.

Ah, night, a glowing pile of shifting color,
Just the way dreams collapse on bisexual expectations;
I don't expect it to be as it is for a girl,
Able to slap after having kissed.

Because the sea never gives up, they don't know where I am.
Because the sea tells no lies, I don't know where my love is.
She's very close but I feel very lonely:
Catch her, then she's free again.

TRANSLATED BY BURTON RAFFEL AND NURDIN SALAM

GRAVE

Kubur

What you can hear, friend,
Besides the moon slowly skipping,
Is the sound of our last tears

Where the dawn of death is for him,
And the world
Rises dark and is silently swallowed.

TRANSLATED BY DERWENT MAY

Bachtiar

NOCTURNO

Nokturno

When my days and times seem so distant, so small,
That all there is to life is the play of light on a fingertip
Come, oh you moments which comfort the soul, and let me
    shine with happiness
As the thin, dull sliver of a moon rushes to transform itself
    into a circle of fire!

When the rainbow of youthful longing hangs in the early
    June glow
I won't remember as far back as those buried loves,
Lying heavily across the flowers that brighten early June.
Come, come!
When I'm myself again I won't have to worry about love's
    flattery, its fake temptations—
Let the menace come at my face, when I'm ready for it,
But you, you come first, oh moments that soothe the body,
When memory never turns to all that's been ruined!

But ah! when there are still things I can ask for
My strength will have escaped from my lips
And my days and times will seem distant again,
Will be distant again.

TRANSLATED BY BURTON RAFFEL AND NURDIN SALAM

ON THE SUBJECT OF FREEDOM

Tentang Kemerdekaan

FOR NAR

Freedom, it's the country and the sea of all its voices:
Don't be afraid of it.

Freedom, it's the poet's country, and the wanderer's:
Don't be afraid of me.

Freedom, it's a deep, devoted love:
Bring me to it.

TRANSLATED BY BURTON RAFFEL AND NURDIN SALAM

Bachtiar

DJAKARTA IN THE EVENING

Ibukota Sendja

Earning my daily living, and daily living
With mud-caked coolies and women bathing naked
In the river I love, O city of my heart.
Bells on the trams and motor-horns competing.
Air weighing on the long and twisting road.

Buildings and heads, lost in the dusk, breaking apart.
Kites like coal in the south-west sky.
                              O city I love,
Press me into the center of your heart,
Into the heart of your noise and of your suffering.

I look up as though I dreamed at a white moon
Swimming in a sky of young clouds.
                              The pure wells
Lie hidden. Earth has its coat of dust.
And hand and word restrain the breath of the free spirit
Waiting to be taken by death.

I know nothing.
                  But outside, all is simple.
Longing songs that play with their own sadness
Wait for the silence surprised at the door at dawn
And the dreams of men go on for ever.

Constantly changing place, the noises of bell and horn,
In the earning one's daily living, and daily living,
Among the coolies returning along the roads,
And women climbing the banks of the river I love.

Bachtiar

The children swimming and laughing in their innocence,
In reflections of the palace seized by cramp.
The evening kites soaring out of sight
In the black night that suddenly leaps out.

The pure wells irretrievably hidden.
The constant coat of dust upon the earth.
Weapon and hand restraining the free spirit.
O city that I love, after the dusk,
City that I live in, and of my longing.

TRANSLATED BY DERWENT MAY

Samiati Alisjahbana

BORN on March 15, 1930, in Djakarta, Samiati Alisjahbana is the daughter of S. T. Alisjahbana (see Part I). After graduating from upper middle school (SMA) she continued her studies at the University of London, 1951–1952, and thereafter in the United States, at Cornell University. She received a Master's degree in anthropology from the latter institution.

Miss Alisjahbana, who is married and the mother of one child, has worked with the Indonesian delegations in New York City and in Paris. Since 1955 she has worked in the Press Section of the Ministry of Foreign Affairs, and has taught both at the University of Indonesia and at Pantjasila University, in Padang, Sumatra. In 1963 she took a leave from her Ministry of Foreign Affairs post in order to manage the publishing house of *Pustaka Rakjat*, established and long directed by her father.

Writing very little, she has published even less; those of her poems which can be dated are from the 1940's, several having been published in the January, 1948, issues of *Mimbar Indonesia*. I am informed that she is no longer publishing her poetry.

QUIET WATER

Air Tenang

Quiet, only tiny ripples.
A fallen leaf drifts,
Following the wind-driven water.
A dragon-fly slowly settles
On the barely-moving leaf.
Dragon-fly-skipper on a ship of leaf
You sail calmly straight by.

.   .   .   .

As if the soul were that calm,
Weakly surrendering to this world
Without a protesting motion, not fighting its loneliness,
As if satisfied—and with just this.
And everything will always be just this way,
Only the muddy soil sinking invisibly deeper.

TRANSLATED BY BURTON RAFFEL AND NURDIN SALAM

Alisjahbana

Part IV

ANGKATAN BARU

The New Generation

W(*illibrordus*) S. Rendra

BORN on November 7, 1935, in Solo, Java, Rendra was brought up in a family environment where artistic matters were of lively concern. His mother had been a dancer, in the traditional Javanese style known as *serimpi;* his father taught Indonesian and Old Javanese at the Solo high school. A student at Gadjah Mada University, in Jogjakarta, studying in the Fakultas Sastra Barat (Faculty of Western Arts), Rendra has written short stories and essays as well as poetry, and has served as a reviewer for both theatrical performances and exhibitions of painting. He has become more and more concerned with the theater, writing and translating plays, acting in them, and directing them. Working with the drama group Artis Teater, in Jogjakarta, he translated and performed Hochwalder's "Das Heilige Experiment" and Sophocles' "Oedipus Rex" (in which he played Oedipus). According to *Cultural News from Asia* (New Delhi, April, 1963, p. 2), "Rendra's group has in petto plays by Christopher Fry, Eugene Ionesco and S. Vincent Benét."

In a letter to a Djakarta friend, Rendra explained his decision to avoid the capital city:

> At first I wanted to study in Djakarta. But then it seemed to me that in Djakarta I might not be able to go on writing poetry. In Djakarta people write poetry because they've been discussing and debating, and out of intellectual excitement. I write poetry because of my own feelings and experiences. And those feelings and experiences must be the sort that push you along your own path. You can do that only by yourself, and not according to some intellectual's opinions. For those reasons I didn't feel like traveling far off, getting myself involved in big city life; I made up my mind, once and for all, to rely on leaves, mountains, and river water. So I'm happier in Jogja.

I have translated this passage from Dick Hartoko's "Gema Suara Alam" (Echoes from Nature), a review article on Rendra's second book of poems, in *Basis*, December, 1961, p. 83. The letter, first published in 1955, in *Merdeka* (Freedom), captures and confirms some of the modest, intensely sympathetic aura of his poetry. And the following, from a letter written—in English—to Bonnie R. Crown, February, 1964, indicates the degree to which (like Chairil Anwar) he is one who has been chosen by poetry, rather than one who chooses:

> I will continue to write poetry. Don't you worry about it. I just cannot help writing poetry. There is always an inner urgency in me to speak to other people beautifully, truthfully, and freely—which means to write poetry. Meanwhile I cannot leave the theatre, too. It is a kind of polygamy. I have been married to poetry and yet I am married again to theatre. . . . I cannot understand fully why I got into this polygamy. It is a mystery of vocation. . . . I [had] always refused to become a poet. . . . I refuse. I refuse. I refuse. Until I cannot refuse anymore. . . . Of course, there is still sometimes the doubt. But the doubt is always overcome. . . .

Rendra's work is unlike anything else I know of in Indonesian, long-limbed, one moment magically descriptive, the next mystical, and then becoming tautly, warmly dramatic. With his brilliant imagery and open sensibility, he seems to me potentially the beginning of vastly exciting things.

Rendra is a Catholic.

Ballada Orang-orang Tertjinta (Lovers' Ballads), 1957; *Empat Kumpulan Sadjak* (Four Groups of Poems), 1961.

138

BALLAD OF THE KILLING OF ATMO KARPO

Ballada Terbunuhnja Atmo Karpo

With its steel hooves the horse thrashes the earth's belly.
The treacherous moon strokes her body above the world.
The fugitive robber thrusts his knees into his steed,
Sodden with stinking sweat, his sword naked.

All the men of the village are out surrounding the forest.
Atmo Karpo is coming home in an eddy of air—
Cursing the womanish moon and his unhappy fortune—
Sprinkling flowers of fire, his left arm pierced by an arrow.

One by one those who step forth are drained of their blood.
The horse and its steel rider go on their own way.

"You have souls to be sold in the market, you feeble-minded!
Your spears are like young leaves—I am far from death in
    this place!
Djoko Pandan! Step forward wherever you are!
It is to you alone I carry my crimes."

Arrows from four directions, enemies on three roads,
The seven-holed body of Atmo Karpo is still upright.

"Djoko Pandan! Step forward wherever you are!
It is to you alone I carry my crimes."

His belly is lying open, yet he is still a demon,
He snarls at his horse, his head droops to the horse's rhythm.

"Djoko Pandan! Step forward wherever you are!
It is to you alone I carry my crimes."

Rendra   *139*

To a ringing neigh from his horse, Djoko Pandan is there!
All yields before the step of his black horse.
His breast is ready to take the roar of his rising hatred.

At the first step the two are men of the same steel.
At the third step Atmo Karpo lies on the ground,
His wounds hot, his flesh spread like the sheath of a leaf.

The night is like a black mask pock-marked with wounds.
The moon is dancing with jubilation, her wine is blood!

Djoko Pandan rises, his sword is shining with blood.
He has killed his father.

TRANSLATED BY DERWENT MAY

KOJAN THE UNFORTUNATE

Kojan Jang Malang

Fire has gutted the forest:
Charred logs curse at the sky
That runs across the world.

Overhead, the moon, shining with blood,
Drips orange tears from its eyes.

Kojan! Kojan!
Sick boy,
What grief is there in you?

Has she come from her dark nest,
The bent crone with her traps and snares?
(The red earth gives off a stench
And the bent crone arrives,
Riding a ball of fog.)

Kojan! Kojan!
Sick boy,
What hate is there in you?

(She steals his leaden heart,
Loots the flowers from his eyes,
And there's nothing he can say!)

Kojan! Kojan!
Overhead, the moon, shining with blood,
Drips orange tears from its eyes,
And now I know:
It's you in her bowels!

TRANSLATED BY BURTON RAFFEL

Rendra

BALLAD OF THE WANDERER

Ballada Petualang

—Is there water still in the old well?
—Yes, fine, yes yes . . .
—Is your brother's wedding arranged now?
—Yes, fine, yes yes . . .

Two crows fly across his path.
Gazing ahead with distant eyes
He walks along with his own words.

Mama, how small he is!
Walking all alone.

—They say that everything's dark in the house.
—Yes, fine, yes yes . . .
—There are no trees or fruit on the road.
—Yes, fine, yes yes . . .

Striding, striding on,
Homesick with every step.
His purpose held tight in his arms
He does not want to turn.

Mama, how straight he is!
He bends to pick up from the road
A tamarind lying there.
How he sucks the shrunken fruit!

—They talk about two graves in the hills.
—Yes, fine, yes yes . . .
—The boy has left the house of heirlooms.
—Yes, fine, yes yes . . .

Rendra

Because the beats of his heart will be cursed
He cannot now go back again.
He goes on to receive his fate.

The village that has lost its color
Speaks to its neighbors:
Why does that good boy
Not turn back again?

TRANSLATED BY DERWENT MAY

Rendra

BALLAD OF THE MEN
OF THE LIMESTONE SOIL

Ballada Lelaki-laki Tanah Kapur

The men have gone into the street,
Their swords tipped with lightning,
And the horses of the robbers
Can be seen on the yellow hilltop.
Blood is the speech now.

Behind barricaded doors
Weep children, pray women.

Without victory there is no word "home."
The coward will lie in the courtyard
And his wife will not open the door.

The beat of hooves draws near
And the wind begins to sing:
"I shall tap the blood of men
From the steel jars of their breasts.
Like generous dealers in wine
The men will lie in the street,
Opened by howling wolves.
O thriving down of the breast!
Garden of sweet vines!"

Half way round the stockade
Spreads the beat of the hooves.
Then the cry of combat,
Men drawing life from their swords,
The spread of a stinking liquid,
Mouths foaming and dust in wounds.

At the third cry of the cockerel
And the first blue light in the sky
The men go back to the village,
Erect with their wounds flowering,
Red gashes and opened breasts.

The door is marked with sweat.

"Who knocks?"

"Your man has come home, faithful woman!"

The women stream from the doors
To lick the wounds of their men.
The girls chant in the windows.

The headman of Kudo Seto,
Like a flower famed for its sap,
Slowly runs his hand
Over his red body.

And at the door of the hut
His wife clings to his feet
While to his son he says:
"Only child of mine,
I bring the sword of the lord of robbers to give to you,
Fastened in the flesh of my right breast!"

TRANSLATED BY DERWENT MAY

THE PROUD CHILD

Anak Jang Angkuh

How cold the river water.
The cold! The cold!
How cold the unhappy flesh
Wrapped around my bones.

Hey, child!
Don't lean against the tree then.
Come in, child!
How cold it is out there!

(Outside the house the wind dances in circles.
The child rubs his bottom and his back.
His father's blows have raised the hatred in him.)

He is still so very little.
His little heart is swollen.
His little fist is raised.
Oh, oh! the little hero
On the edge of the river of blood.

Hey, child!
Eyes like coal glowing in the wind.
Come in, child!
How cold it is out there!

(The tiny leaves are falling
And dropping on his hair.
He sticks out his chest,
The proud little animal.)

Rendra

Oh, oh! and how he snivels.
Why must a man be proud,
Drinking praise and conceit,
Heated by dirty blood?

Hey, child!
Your father's blood is in your sinews.
Smile and your father will be meek again.
This spirit is like your own.
One smile will not make mockery of your anger.
Come in, child!
How cold it is out there!

(Under a black silk sky,
With broken twigs at his feet,
The child swells out his chest,
Head raised, and how great his pride!)

TRANSLATED BY DERWENT MAY

BALLAD OF THE CRUCIFIXION

Ballada Penjaliban

Jesus walks to Golgotha
Carrying a wooden cross,
Like a lamb with pure white fleece.

There are no roses on the path,
No palm leaves:
A white lamb struggling under torment and whips,
Bent by a duty dearly loved
And rooted in desire.

The sun makes
His wounds drip,
And our father Abraham
Kneels, his hands raised to the Father
—Our Father in Heaven,
Who has sacrificed this whitest lamb
On the highest of altars.
Our Father in Heaven,
Send us the rainbow!

He strides toward Golgotha,
His heart exalted and bright,
Swallowing sin after sin,
Swallowed no matter how bitter.

There are no cloaks spread on the path;
His mother weeps, her hair stained with dust;
And all the women in the city share her weeping.

—Women!
Why do you weep for me
And not for yourselves?

Red rosewater drips from His body
Sprinkling the dry road,
The winding path of a soul in torment,
And the slaughter goes on,
Evil receiving its prize.

The wine which is His blood will pour from His side,
Will come to His lips in a golden cup,
And He will die, poisoned
—Father, let it be finished!

TRANSLATED BY BURTON RAFFEL

LOVE LETTER

Surat Tjinta

I'm writing this letter
While the rain drizzles like a toy
Drum played by magic children
In some magic world.
And the wind sighs,
Puffs and sighs.
Hey, little sister Narti,
I love you!

I'm writing this letter
While the sky drips down
And two small wild ducks
Are making love in the pond
Like two naughty children,
Funny and nice,
Two flapping ducks
Making their feathers shake.
Hey, little sister Narti,
I want you for my wife!

The rain's quick step
Patters along the ground.
Like gleaming, heavy metal
Love walks steadily
Forward,
Never turns back.

Twelve angels
Have descended,
In this time of drizzling rain:
In front of the window-mirror
They stare and wash their hair

For the celebration.
Hey, little sister Narti,
In my fancy bridegroom clothes,
Covered with flowers and wearing a sacred sword,
I ache to lead you to the altar
And marry you.

I asked for you.
You knew I would, long ago:
No one else is worse
Or better . . . . . .
I'm a poet of small, ordinary things,
I began with words,
And words begin
With life, and thought, and feeling.

The sweet strong pleasure of life
Like a million tiny needles
Prickling through the sky:
A blessing of gold at the end of the rainbow.
Then the rain poured down.
Love and the wind

Sigh helplessly in the drizzle.
The sweet strong pleasure of my love,
Like a thousand invisible hands
Spreading a thousand nets,
Pounces on your heart
That smiles so steadily at me.

You're a mermaid princess
And my captive.
Mermaid, with
Your voice as gentle
As a sea breeze,
Sigh for me!
The wind sighs
And sighs
A clear sweet lament.

Rendra   *151*

You're a mermaid princess,
Turning softly,
Blinking your beautiful eyes
In my net.
Oh mermaid princess,
I've caught you,
I've asked for you.

I'm writing this letter
While rain drips
From the sky;
A sweet, spoiled child
Cries for her toys;
Two mischievous little boys
Are having fun in the ditch
And the jealous sky is watching.
Hey, little sister Narti,
I want you
To be the mother of my children!

TRANSLATED BY BURTON RAFFEL

Ajip Rossidhy

BORN on January 31, 1938, in Djatiwangi, Java, Rossidhy
(or Rosidi) is the youngest poet represented in this volume.
At the age of thirteen he was writing for his school magazine; he has gone on writing—poetry, short stories, novels,
criticism—at a furious pace ever since, mostly in Indonesian
but also in Sundanese. His work has been published widely
and he has himself been on the editorial staffs of several
periodicals. Any judgment of a poet so young and so pro-
lific seems to me decidedly premature. He is strongly romantic—but also, as the masterful self-portrait of adolescence
which follows demonstrates, he is potentially capable of the
artistic discipline still lacking in most of his work.

Pesta (Festivity), 1956; *Ketemu Didjalan* (Met in the
Street), 1956 (with Sebron Aidit and S. M. Ardan); *Tjari
Muatan* (Hunting for Cargo), 1959. The seven-page preface
to *Tjari Muatan*, dated February 24, 1958, is a masterful
self-portrait of the young poet and his arrival in the big city—
naïve, vivid, and fascinating.

ENDAI RASIDIN'S LOVE LETTER

Surattjinta Endaj Rasidin

In the sinking twilight we've walked, you and I,
Into a great kingdom that was sinking too,
Butting in through a low gate that mussed our hair,
Walking with our hands jammed into our pockets—

A country where houses have windows on every side,
A country where houses bathe in the sun,
The country of those I love
In soft, hoarse whispers,
In hoarse, close whispers—

Where everyone laughs and laughs
Even if the light no longer reaches them.

We've walked, you and I, in the brutal sun,
We've walked, you and I, in the dark whirlpool of night,
Meeting in the corner of some hidden hut
In our loose coats and shoes that don't match—

A hut where the roof is as high as my shoulders,
A hut just big enough to stretch out,
The hut of those I love
With wild laughter that has no cause,
With stories that bring on wild laughter—

Where people talk and talk
Even if they run out of words.

Rossidhy

We've walked, you and I, hand in hand,
We've walked one after another
In our trousers rolled to the knee,
In our rakish hats, and our embroidered blue kerchiefs:

Where people laugh and talk,
Where we sink down among them . . . . .

TRANSLATED BY BURTON RAFFEL

Rossidhy

TRANSLATORS

Ahmed Ali

Ahmed Ali edited and introduced *The Flaming Earth: Poems from Indonesia* (Karachi, 1949) for the Friends of the Indonesian Republic Society; he was assisted in his translations by Idham. Professor Ali has also translated from the Chinese and from the Urdu.

Sutan Takdir Alisjahbana

The dean of Indonesian letters, S. T. Alisjahbana is represented in this anthology at pages 33–34; a brief biography is given at that point.

James S Holmes

An American long resident in Amsterdam, James S Holmes was Associate Editor for *Perspective of Indonesia* (1956). He has published translations from and critical discussions of Indonesian literature, including the introduction to *Chairil Anwar: Selected Poems* (New Directions, 1963). Mr. Holmes translates, also, from the Dutch, and is an editor of *Delta: A Review of Arts, Life, and Thought in the Netherlands.*

Idham

Born in Medan, Sumatra, in 1918, Idham received his secondary education in Indonesia, later studying chemistry at Utrecht. In 1947, at the time of his collaboration with Professor Ahmed Ali, he was Indonesian chargé d'affaires in New Delhi. His own writing has appeared in *Het Inzicht* and *De Linie.*

156

Jean Kennedy

Jean Kennedy is a painter and industrial designer. She and her husband have lived (and painted) in Italy; with Frank Lloyd Wright in Taliesin, Wisconsin; in Indonesia, where they spent four years; and they have recently departed from a post in Addis Ababa, Ethiopia, for another in Lagos, Nigeria.

Derwent May

Derwent May spent the years 1955 to 1958 in Indonesia, under the auspices of the British Council, lecturing in English at the University of Indonesia. Himself a poet, Mr. May is acquainted with many of Indonesia's leading writers and literary commentators; he is one of the very few non-Indonesians to have written interpretive criticism of the Indonesian literary scene. Once again under the auspices of the British Council, he recently spent several years in Warsaw, Poland, and is now on the staff of the *Times Literary Supplement*, London. Chatto and Windus are soon to publish his first novel.

Burton Raffel

Resident in Indonesia from 1953 to 1955, as an instructor in the Ford Foundation English Language Teacher Training Program, Burton Raffel has published poetry, fiction, and three previous volumes of verse translation: *Poems from the Old English, Beowulf,* and *Chairil Anwar: Selected Poems,* the last in collaboration with Nurdin Salam. Together with Professor James N. Mosel, he is preparing an anthology of Thai poetry. Mr. Raffel has lectured on, given readings of, and written critical commentary about Indonesian poetry; assisted by a grant from the American Philosophical Society, he is writing a history of Indonesian poetry, incorporating many new translations (including samples of Indonesian literary-critical prose).

157

Nurdin Salam

Born in 1931, educated and continuously resident in Makassar, Nurdin Salam spent many years as a civil servant while completing his English language studies. Burton Raffel was one of his teachers: they have been collaboratively translating Indonesian poetry since 1954. Having now qualified as an *ahli bahasa Inggeris* (English language expert), Mr. Salam is studying for his Master's degree.

Sabina Thornton

Sabina Thornton, as a student at the University of California, prepared English language versions of a number of Indonesian poems, working from drafts supplied her by S. T. Alisjahbana, who was then in residence at the Center for Advanced Study in the Behavioral Sciences, Stanford University, California.